African Markets and the Utu-Ubuntu Business Model

A Perspective on Economic Informality in Nairobi

Mary Njeri Kinyanjui

AFRICAN MINDS

Published in 2019 by African Minds
4 Eccleston Place, Somerset West 7130, Cape Town, South Africa
info@africanminds.org.za
www.africanminds.org.za

ISBN Paper 978-1-928331-78-0
ISBN eBook 978-1-928331-79-7
ISBN ePub 978-1-928331-80-3

Orders
African Minds
4 Eccleston Place, Somerset West 7130, Cape Town, South Africa
info@africanminds.org.za
www.africanminds.org.za

For orders from outside South Africa:
African Books Collective
PO Box 721, Oxford OX1 9EN, UK
orders@africanbookscollective.com
www.africanbookscollective.com

Culture plays a central role in the political, economic and social life of communities. Indeed, culture may be the missing link in the development of Africa. Culture is dynamic, evolves over time, consciously discarding retrogressive traditions, like female genital mutilation, and embracing aspects that are good and useful. Africans, especially, should rediscover the positive aspects of their culture. In accepting them, they would give themselves a sense of belonging, identity and self-confidence.

– Wangari Maathai, Nobel Lecture, 2004

For my teachers. In the true spirit of utu-ubuntu, they selflessly taught and prepared me for the Great Transformation in my life. Yet, when the self-regulating market and money culture became entrenched in Kenya, they were among the first to be alienated and impoverished.

Contents

List of plates

Acknowledgements

I benefited from the generosity and care of many people while I was writing this book. I shared ideas with my Comparative Industrial Strategy class at the University of Nairobi's Institute for Development Studies. Their critique challenged me to think more deeply about traders and artisans in Nairobi.

Fredrick Dawa, secretary of the Kamukunji Jua Kali Association in Nairobi, was a source of inspiration and ideas, probing me to delve into the experiences of traders and artisans. I held numerous fruitful discussions about the nature and organisation of markets with Pastor Kihara and Mrs Wakagiri of Uhuru Market. John Ng'ang'a, chairperson of the Uhuru Market Traders Association, was also a source of information on the role of markets.

Ignatius Gacheru and Philomena Njeri Mbari helped me understand and explain the Agikuyu business ethos. Gitu wa Kahengeri, the secretary-general of the Mau Mau War Veterans Association, gave me insights into the socio-economic expectations of Kenya's freedom struggle. Charles Rubia, Nairobi's first mayor, provided information on efforts he made to transform Nairobi from a colonial outpost into an African city; Njogu Wanguu also provided historical information about Nairobi, while Deborah Kinuthia, Richard Gitau and Edith Muhindi shared the experiences of their families in Nairobi.

Muraguri Nguyai, Mark Kamau, George Kamau, Francis Kinuthia, Martin Njoroge, Linet Muracha, Stephene Kingoina, Pauline Wambua, Perpetua Ng'ang'a and Rachel Waweru helped in gathering data in the markets. Sam Balongo helped with data management and analysis while Boniface Ngaruia and Josephat Juma read the draft manuscripts.

Dr Paul Kamau taught my classes when I went on two writing retreats for this book. I am grateful to Prof. Winnie Mitullah, Director of the Institute for Development Studies at the University of Nairobi, and to the university itself for giving me leave to attend these retreats. I am also grateful to my former students, Victor Kibet, Pauline Wambua, David Mbuvi, Stephen King'oina and Francis Kinuthia, who offered valuable ideas during brainstorming sessions for the book, and to Fredrick Gitonga for taking photographs. Stephene Kariuki drove me around while Richard Ambani helped with archival materials.

My friends Anne Kamau, Joy Obando, Belta Makato, Lydia Kamau, Angela Kamau, Nguyai Mbari, Boniface Njenga, Marjory Kimani, Anne Kariuki, Lydia Gaitirira, Anne Njuguna, Faith Kimathi, Boniface Ngaruia, Reverend David Mwakiwiwi, Felix Kiruthu, Wanjiru Gichuhi, Eunice Wanjoya and Francis Kanyoni were a source of encouragement in many ways. Three of my former lecturers, Agnes Musyoki, Michael Darkoh and Celia Nyamweru, always show an interest in my writing for which I am most grateful. Josephat Juma has read several drafts of this work and given feedback. Emmanuel Gitau and his wife arranged and accompanied me to my interview with Gitu wa Kahengeri.

I am also heavily indebted to my family. They were always available to cheer me up when I was in doubt, exhausted and wondering whether I could complete a chapter. Mungai, Josephine and Shiru Kamiti responded to my emails and telephone calls with encouragement. Jane Wairimu and her family were always ready to run my errands and manage my affairs. Lydia Wairimu and Anastacia Gatherero, together with their families, supported me immensely. Josephine Muthoni and her family also provided useful support. My mother constantly reminded me to take care of my health and avoid sitting for long hours. My father always encouraged me to do my best and accept the fact that things will not always work in my favour. My brothers and their families are always a source of support. I am also grateful to Dr Pius Kigamwa for listening to my stories and reminding me to set realistic goals. My daughter Mercy Nyambura supported me in more ways than I can say.

The Stellenbosch Institute for Advanced Study (STIAS) offered me two writing residencies. During the first, I wrote two chapters and presented some of my work at a seminar during which I received helpful comments from others. The second residency was unfortunately cut short due to personal circumstances. My thanks to Simon Bekker as well as Sandra and Maria Mouton, who offered me their friendship during my time at STIAS. I am also grateful to the Rockefeller Foundation's Bellagio Center for a month-long resident fellowship during which I wrote the concluding chapter and presented my work to other fellows who also made useful comments. The fellowships at STIAS and the Bellagio Center gave me the support and inspiration to really focus on writing.

Preface

I wrote this book to try to resolve some of the contradictions I have experienced as a student, a practitioner and also a subject of economic informality, urbanisation and development. As a student of development in the 1980s and 1990s, I was exposed to Karl Polanyi's idea that development involves a 'great transformation' of social, cultural and economic ways of life, and that this is brought about through the establishment of self-regulating markets, the entrenchment of a money culture and the adoption of a new religion and formal education. Apparently, in Africa, the first steps towards this transformation were taken during the colonial period and further progress is being made by postcolonial states via the neoliberal policies they have since adopted.

I also learned that African culture presents certain obstacles to this transformation process. Punitive attitudes towards gender apparently prevent women from participating fully in economic activities while the fact that individualism and competition are generally discouraged supposedly suppresses entrepreneurship and innovation. So, to benefit from the great transformation, Africans are often advised to adopt the individualist mindset that will allow them to embrace economic competition, self-regulating markets, as well as new farming methods.

In the early 1990s, while reading for my doctorate at the

University of Cambridge in the United Kingdom, I realised that some of the prescriptions geared towards spurring economic growth in Africa – such as those directed at peasant farmers growing coffee in my village – were, in fact, perpetuating complex systems of exploitation. In 1997, in a bid to own a home in Nairobi, I began constructing a house in Kahawa Sukari on the outskirts of the city. This entailed hiring and sourcing materials from traders and artisans in the informal economy.

My transition from being a researcher on economic informality to being a consumer and participant in the informal economy gave me a deeper understanding and appreciation of the complexities and intricacies of this world. My perception of traders and artisans as hapless individuals, lacking in capital and entrepreneurial skills, changed completely. I soon saw them as people who knew their business well and commanded strong networks. They shared their business experiences with me in ways that they would not have done had I been a mere researcher. Their stories helped me to begin to conceptualise economic informality as an alternative business model and led me to research and write about this as I have done over the past several years.

Since independence, Kenya's postcolonial governments have tried to play 'catch-up' by creating policies and institutions similar to those behind economic and development planning in Europe, North America and East Asia. In other words, the Kenyan government has been trying to replicate the great transformation that took place in Europe in the 19th century, which involved the establishment of so-called self-regulating markets and the growth of large corporations. Of course, such transformation has remained elusive in Africa, and Kenya is no exception. In my view, part of the reason why transformation has failed is because interventions by the state and corporations have either ignored the economic role and contribution of indigenous traders and artisans (who have accumulated capital and developed their own methods of doing business) or demanded that these groups abandon their own business strategies and adopt those acceptable to self-regulating markets instead. Traders and artisans have consistently resisted this.

In the Kenyan context, one of the earliest forms of resistance to the great transformation was expressed in one of my paternal grandmother's favourite songs, *Mbia ciokire* (When money was introduced). The song decries the ways in which money alienates people from their humanity and undermines the values of solidarity, caring and nurturing in families, affecting relations between husbands and wives, mothers and sons. The song reflects the fact that prior to the colonial invasion, African communities placed the values of humanity and solidarity at the centre of production and exchange. These values served as the basis for mutual generosity and reciprocity. In contemporary Kenya, a similar view is expressed in another song, *Shilingi yaua tena maua* (A shilling is a beautiful flower but it kills), which challenges the entrenchment of neoliberalism, which values wealth above all.

Although resistance to the veneration of money is well-enough embedded in local culture that songs are regularly composed about it, this is seldom mentioned in analyses of African economies. Nevertheless, many Africans have resisted the great transformation. Rotating credit or savings associations such as susu in West Africa, chama in Kenya and stokvels in South Africa are one example of this resistance. Another key example, that is explored and examined in depth in this book is the efforts of traders and artisans to sustain the institution of African markets.

Despite enduring more than a century of disruption, first by colonial conquest and now by globalisation, African markets persist as complex and autonomous communities of exchange and production. They are spaces in which communities harness their agency to sustain and renew a network of households, some of which traverse the urban–rural divide, and which rely on flows of skills and resources that are largely independent of the formal economy.

Another popular song, *Mucibi wa marigiti* (The market belt), depicts markets in Nairobi as spaces in which traders have the power to survive and then thrive. In the song, the composer pays tribute to his mother who, by trading at the market, raises enough money to educate her son. He later acquires a job and reciprocates by building her a house. The composer acknowledges he was once ashamed that his mother was not more affluent but now can appreciate how much his own success relied on what she was able to achieve as a trader. The song substantiates the notion that African markets empower people to harness their agency to perform the dual roles of economic production and domestic reproduction. In this process, the markets sustain traders' sense of their own power as well as that of their families and communities. The tightening of the market belt can be seen as symbolic of a business model that entails resilience, hope, education, solidarity generosity, and reciprocity.

I call this mode of transaction the utu-ubuntu business model. *Utu* is a Swahili word meaning 'humanness' and *ubuntu* is a Zulu word for 'solidarity'. As a philosophy, utu-ubuntu serves many purposes in the social and economic realms of many communities in Africa. It rests on the principle that all human beings are interconnected and interdependent. It refutes and resists Western culture's exaltation of individualism and its veneration of wealth and technology as solutions to human problems. Instead, it affirms African culture by advocating and perpetuating the values of communality and reciprocity. For this reason, utu-ubuntu has been described as offering a workable model for restoring social and economic justice (Tutu 1999).

As a business model, utu-ubuntu acknowledges that all economic transactions are embedded in social relations. From this perspective, the main purpose of doing business is to build and sustain the autonomous and self-regulating networks that one belongs to. For example, traders and artisans in Nairobi share operational costs related to transport, security and space. They also share their knowledge through exchanging stories about their experiences. They engage in a kind of 'crowd-funding' – pooling their income to pay for capital investments or social insurance. Most of this activity is based on principles of reciprocity and sharing that weave individuals into a net of shared personal, social and religious ties. The model is inclusive and seldom leaves traders in debt.

Using this utu-ubuntu model to understand the activities of traders and artisans, I explore how, despite being consistently excluded and disadvantaged, they have shaped urban spaces in and around Nairobi and contributed to the development of the city as a whole. With immense resilience, and without discarding their own socio-cultural or economic values, they have formed a territorial complex that I refer to as the African metropolis.

For me, the term 'African metropolis' refers to those parts of many African cities that have been established on the basis of African logic and according to the norms of self-sufficiency and self-determination. In these areas, places have African names, the work of traders and artisans is often the dominant mode of production, and individuals are closely connected to their neighbours and to the broader community via a range of kinship and other ties. In contemporary Kenyan slang, these areas are referred to as *kijiji* (villages), and they are substantially different to Nairobi's more affluent neighbourhoods (which bear English names), such as Westlands, Parklands and Lavington. In my view, if this utu-ubuntu way of doing business were to be mainstreamed and used to inform national economic and urban planning, inclusive and sustainable urban development might stand a chance. I therefore conclude the book with a brief discussion of how such villages could be enhanced and extended.

Chapter 1

Introduction

Traders and artisans are a popular feature of Africa's city streets and marketplaces. To an outsider, they may appear haphazard and constantly changing. However, sustained observation quickly reveals that this impression is far from valid, and prompts many questions. What motivates traders and artisans to go into business? How do they relate to one another? Why do they congregate? How do they handle conflict? Do they make a profit? How do they spend their earnings? How is the market managed? Which transactions are carried out openly and which are private? Do traders have any collective power and, if so, how do they use it? What philosophies, ideologies and social formations prevail in the marketplaces?

Scholarly works on African markets by Grabski (2012), Harris (2014) and Ikioda (2013) offer diverse responses to some of these questions. Grabski describes African markets as spaces of creativity. Her study of Colobane Market in Dakar, Senegal, demonstrates how the market has affected the artistic imaginary of local artists. Ikioda describes markets in Lagos as communities of practice that create employment, prompt income generation and act as spaces that connect the rural and urban areas. Harris, however, describes markets as messy 'agglomeration economies' characterised by intense competition that jeopardises innovation and growth.

In this book, I traverse these perspectives and try to describe:

i) the nature of past and present social formations that have influenced marketplaces in Nairobi; ii) the logics and philosophies that underpinned and influenced their formation and which continue to do so; iii) the relationships between traders and artisans, including how they share knowledge and how rules and regulations are formed; and iv) how markets have shaped the city by attracting and sustaining a labour pool and via traders' investment of their surplus income.

I show that the transactions, practices and notions of business that predominate in African markets intimate the presence of humanistic values, such as solidarity, humanity, endurance, trust and sharing. The textbook model of business, as necessarily involving aggression, competition, secrecy and self-individuation, does not seem to apply here. To survive, traders and artisans have evolved a business model that operates on the basis of humanity and solidarity, and that helps them harness their own agency through the sharing of experience and through self-regulation. This model assumes that business transactions between individuals are embedded in both a sense of community and an awareness of the divine. The utu-ubuntu approach holds that the main reason for the accumulation and deployment of surplus is to help families and communities to thrive. As a result, the markets sustain autonomous communities that have the resources to advance their own interests in ways that have shaped the evolution and sprawl of the metropolis itself.

For some, the idealistic and moralistic undertones inherent in the term 'utu-ubuntu' might be controversial. In the late 1960s, then-president of Tanzania Julius Nyerere attempted to promote the philosophy of utu through the policy of ujamaa but failed. The failure was occasioned by ujamaa's association with socialism in the context of the Cold War. Nevertheless, utu remains at the heart of the organisation and distribution of resources in most African communities. Similarly, the Marikana massacre and the shockingly inadequate services often delivered by many of South Africa's government departments have made the reality of ubuntu in that country highly questionable. Yet, the notion remains one that many South Africans hold dear and try to live up to.

While civil conflict, poor governance and state corruption challenge the usefulness of utu-ubuntu as a development strategy in Africa, these factors are, in my view, symptomatic less of the failure of utu-ubuntu and more of the unwillingness of African elites to embrace the values on which utu and ubuntu are based. The values of utu-ubuntu do not assume or suggest that African societies or communities are, or ever were, conflict free. The Rwandan genocide alone is sufficient proof of this. However, it can be argued that, by rejecting the values of sharing, community service, care, respect, honesty and trustworthiness, the African elite are entrenching bad governance and corruption, and ultimately fuelling conflict. Certainly, few members of the elite seem to have been socialised into the philosophy of utu-ubuntu. They appear ignorant of the benefits of connecting with ordinary people, of sharing resources, of resilience and the benefits of harnessing their agency for the good of others.

The role of traders and artisans in the evolution of cities tends to be disregarded and discounted by academics and policy-makers. Studied under the rubric of the informal sector, traders and artisans are perceived as barely subsisting in precarious conditions. According to Ferguson (2013: 231), 'what goes on in the (misleadingly named) "informal economy" is less about producing goods and services than it is about finding opportunities for…"distributive labour"'. For such scholars, the existence of traders and artisans is evidence that African economies have failed to achieve what European historian and political economist Karl Polanyi (1944) famously describes as the great transformation that happened in Europe in the 19th century and more recently in East Asia with the rise of the market economy.

According to Polanyi, the changes that occurred in Europe, and which formed the foundation of today's global economies, entailed the displacement and dislocation of peasants and artisans by firms and corporations. This gave rise to large-scale urbanisation, the emergence of a money culture and the so-called self-regulating market, which, in turn, generated a footloose labour force that is vulnerable to exploitation by large corporations.

In most of Africa, this kind of transformation has not occurred. Why most African countries failed to undergo a great transformation in the 19th century, or to embrace the economics of flexible specialisation in the 20th century, remain questions for some. As Mitra et al. (2017) observe, postcolonial capitalism is overwhelmingly dominated by informality. Peasants, artisans and traders dominate the economic landscape and accumulation occurs in non-conventional spaces, such as households, where enterprising and self-sufficient communities are nurtured. Added to this, a consistently negative discourse has left traders and artisans excluded from calculations of gross domestic product, from national statistics on employment and from allocations of state resources.

Despite neglect and exclusion from the dominant economic paradigm, traders and artisans epitomise resilience and resist domination as they endeavour to engage in business and earn a living. Their resilience is reflected in their ability to stay afloat in environments characterised by local and multinational corporate competition, and in which the political and economic elites use their influence to favour foreign direct investment via subsidies and policy biases. Their resistance is reflected in their efforts to preserve African logic, values and norms in their business practices. As Ndi (2007) observes, a major marker of postcolonial African cities was the emergence of what are often termed 'informal economies'. In effect, informal economies are alternative modes of production, based on indigenous traditions, practices and notions of place. In many African cities, they have prevented the imperial idea of metropolitan areas (as shaped and dominated by corporate capitalism) from taking root (Ndi 2007).

Many have tried to analyse what makes freedom, autonomy and independence thrive. Classical urban theory, in both its liberal and Marxian forms, tends to view cities as spaces in which human freedom, autonomy and independent agency should prevail (see Lefebvre 1974/1991; Parker 2004; Simmel 1903/2002). Similarly, Scott (2011) suggests that by combining individual enterprise with free-market forces, industrial capitalism has been the magic wand behind the evolution of cities in Europe and North America. From this perspective, Africa is the only continent on which industrial capitalism has not been a motive force for urbanisation. As a result, African urbanisation is often classified as dysfunctional and seen as plagued by a dearth of formal economic activity. African cities are described as 'stragglers or failures' (Bekker & Fourchard 2013: 1). Yet, while some hope that Africa might provide yet another frontier for the growth of urban-based industrial capitalism (see Giugale 2014 for example), industrial capital is, in fact, in deep crisis as a result of environmental pillage and climate change.

In fact, traders, artisans and economic informality operating outside of the dominant modern economic paradigm continue to prevail in African cities. According to an International Labour Organization (ILO) report, titled *Women and Men in the Informal Economy* (ILO 2002), approximately 70% of people living in African cities work in the informal sector. A report by the Kenya National Bureau of Statistics (KNBS 2014) notes that two-thirds of Nairobi's three million inhabitants were employed in the informal sector, and that this sector was the largest creator of jobs nationally.

Can traders and artisans serve as alternative drivers for urban development? In my view, these groups have always been a major factor in the emergence and spatial development of many African cities. They have accomplished this using their utu-ubuntu business model, achieving very different results from those produced by factory floors, Fordist firms and the post-Fordist information economies that have shaped urbanisation in Europe, North America and East Asia.

I address four main questions in this book: i) Do African traders and artisans have a business model? ii) What contributes to the resilience of traders and artisans in African cities? iii) How have traders and artisans shaped the evolution of Africa's cities? iv) Could the acknowledgement, acceptance and expansion of traders' and of artisans' business models have a positive impact on their livelihoods, and on the evolution of safer and healthier African cities in which resources are more equitably allocated?

Why am I concerned with what traders and artisans in marketplaces have to offer to Africa's cities in this digital age, when the African middle class is growing and massive shopping malls are springing up like invasive alien vegetation? The answer is partly that many urban dwellers in Africa have yet to feel the impact of the great transformation through either their educational or work experience. In Nairobi, for example, few of the city's more than two million traders and artisans are fully literate (Kinyanjui 2014). Yet, the marketplaces are key to the distribution of goods and services in the city, and a major source of employment. They also form the bedrock of autonomous communities that function on the basis of learning, self-regulation and surplus deployment. The majority of women and recent migrants in Nairobi derive their livelihoods from marketplaces, and a large percentage of people living in the more affluent suburbs, in the villages on the urban peripheries, and in the rural areas, retain close links with traders and artisans in the city.

The African Development Bank observed that 'from 1960 to 2011, the urban share of Africa's population rose from 19–39% – equivalent to just above 416 million people in 2011' (African Development Bank 2014: 7). The cities of Dar es Salaam and Kinshasa are among the fastest growing in the world, and the bank predicted that by 2014 half of Africa's population would live in cities. This rate of urbanisation requires creative, sustainable, innovative and inclusive development. In my view, promoting the activities and sphere of influence of traders and artisans in indigenous African markets is among the most creative and wide-ranging solutions to this massive challenge.

Development planning discourse has largely ignored African indigenous markets. Considered archaic and irrelevant to contemporary development planning (Ikioda 2013), these markets are seen as spaces of disorder (Meagher 2007) and 'uncreative destruction' that are slow in absorbing technological innovation (Harris 2014; McCormick 1999; Schimdtz & Nadvi 1999). Viewed within the paradigm of economic informality, informal markets are depicted as part of a residual sector that remains unarticulated with large capital (Bromley 1978; Moser 1978), as harbouring criminal or illegal activities (De Soto 1989), and as ineffective in providing for the welfare of their participants (ILO 2000). Perceived in these ways, it is not surprising that the promotion and expansion of such markets is seldom encouraged. Indeed, a host of global bodies, such as the ILO, the United Nations Development Programme (UNDP)and Women in Informal Employment: Globalizing and Organizing, see themselves as helping to rescue people who they consider 'trapped' in the informal sector.

In this context, it is important to affirm that traders and artisans are, in fact, part of organised and autonomous communities that have helped harness human agency for urbanisation in countless situations. Indeed, having survived continual marginalisation and exclusion imposed by colonialism, postcolonialism and neoliberalism, markets deserve recognition as offering a legitimate and resilient model for sound urban development.

In Nairobi, traders and artisans were relegated to the margins when they were designated as hawkers under the Metropolitan Act of 1928. When Kenya achieved independence in the mid-1960s, traders and artisans enjoyed a brief reprieve as the city's first African mayor, Charles Rubia, allocated them spaces in which to work. Contemporary Nairobi has 45 marketplaces designated by the city administration to house traders and artisans. Nevertheless, these remain a focus of controversy and are often threatened with demolition (Robertson 1993). They have been utterly neglected by urban planners as viable means of supporting urbanisation (Kinyanjui 2014).

The humanist solidarity promoted by the utu-ubuntu model creates possibilities for equitable (and therefore sustainable) urban development precisely because the model has evolved with so little formal support and so few resources. Nevertheless, it has enabled traders and artisans to harness their agency and claim the dignity, freedom and independence to operate in hostile and repressive urban spaces. This is why the business model should be seriously considered as offering an alternative model of urbanisation.

In some ways, the markets hark back to the traditional societies that Diamond (2012) suggests might offer solutions in today's troubled world. As Diamond (2012: 32–33) observes:

Traditional societies represent thousands of millennia-long natural experiments in organizing human lives. We cannot repeat those experiments by redesigning thousands of societies today in order to wait decades and observe the outcomes; we have to learn from the societies that already ran the experiments.

African traders and artisans offer working examples of how sharing resources and working in solidarity can help individuals and communities to maintain their dignity, independence and freedom in a context of scarce resources. The values that they live and work by act to continually build and cement the family, friendship and ethnic ties. These ties create resilient and autonomous communities that learn from their experiences and follow rules about production and exchange. They generate surpluses which they use to build themselves and their communities. In other words, trader and artisan communities serve as nests for building agency, for evolving and sharing business skills, self-regulation strategies, technical innovations and wealth creation.

As an evolving city, Nairobi exhibits both global and local spatial and cultural forms as well as different business logics, values and norms. Global cultural forms are reflected in the business ethics of multinational corporations and elite African businesses. Socially and culturally, cathedrals, temples, churches, mosques, fitness centres and sports complexes, non-governmental organisations (NGOs) and charity organisations reflect the impact of globalisation in the city – an impact that is mirrored in high-rise buildings, shopping malls, gated communities, highways and superhighways.

My focus is on the spatial and cultural forms that I see as constituting the African metropolis. Spatially, the African metropolis is manifested in Nairobi's indigenous markets in urbanised villages (such as Kikuyu, Riruta, Dagoretti, Kangemi, Kabete, Kinoo and Uthiru) and in *mwananchi* (citizen-developed spaces) such as Githurai, Wendani, Kasarani, Mwiki, Zimmermann, Ngumba and Kahawa. Most of the urbanised villages existed long before colonialism, while the *mwananchi* are part of a phenomenon that began in the late 1970s, intensified in the late 1990s and persisted into the first two decades of the new millennium. They are places where individuals obtain serviced plots and build their own homes. These areas are characterised by a variety of different coloured, shaped and sized structures and the use of a wide range of building materials.

The relationships between the evolution of Nairobi's markets and the African metropolis are close and clear. I return to this in later chapters; for now, let me simply point out that indigenous markets draw their labour and investors from the metropolis, and through the deployment of surplus, these investors contribute to the development and expansion of *both* the African metropolis *and* the rest of the city. The role that traders and artisans have played in driving urbanisation in Nairobi is evident in the many micro and small-scale traders who work in Nairobi's central business district (CBD), making it one large African market (Kinyanjui 2014; Ngwalla 2011). Their presence cannot be ignored and has affected the design of open-plan shops and created many jobs in the CBD.

Parnell and Pieterse (2014) observe that an urban revolution in Africa is affecting leaders, institutions and technical domains related to design, technology and finance. Underpinning this revolution is a new respect for and acknowledgement of exactly the kinds of indigenous values and practices that have always been fundamental to the utu-ubuntu business model and therefore to the growth of the African metropolis. These processes must be better understood and supported if indigenisation is to play an effective role in fostering inclusive growth in African cities.

To delve into the history of indigenisation in Nairobi, I visited the colonial and postcolonial archives to trace the evolution of the city's markets and their impact on the African metropolis. Archival sources reveal ongoing efforts of successive city governments to repress traders and limit their access to trading sites. This is discussed in more detail later in the book.

To find out more about whether traders and artisans have a business model and how their activities impact on urban development, I carried out a survey among 385 traders and 289 artisans drawn from 14 markets in Nairobi (see Table 1). Most of these markets house both traders and artisans. Some, like Gikomba

Market and Stage Market, have links with global trade. Wakulima Market draws its products mainly from East Africa and supplies several other markets. Uhuru Market specialises in garment-making while Kamukunji Market is mainly an artisans' market. No official records are kept on the number of traders and artisans that work at each market but they all accommodate more traders than city planners initially intended.

TABLE 1 *Markets surveyed in Nairobi, 2015*

Market	Primary product range	Traders or artisans
Gikomba	Secondhand clothing, furniture, timber and bag-making	Both
Githurai	Fresh produce, clothing, metalwork and furniture	Both
Kamukunji	Metal goods	Artisans
Kangemi	Fresh produce, furniture, clothing and metalwork	Both
Kariokor	Tourist artefacts including beads, sandals, jewellery and bags	Both
Kawangware	Fresh produce, food, furniture, metalwork and clothing	Both
Kiamaiko	Goat meat and the slaughter of goats	Both
Mutindwa	Clothing, furniture and metalwork	Both
Ruiru	Fresh produce, metalwork and furniture	Both
Stage	Imported clothing and bags	Both
Toy	Secondhand clothing	Both
Uhuru	Clothing and garment-making	Artisans
Wakulima	Fresh produce	Traders
Westlands	Fresh produce	Traders

The survey involved spending time with traders to try to understand their ethics, work and employment practices, rules and regulations, modes of production, where they live, and how they deploy their income. The survey questions were designed to reveal if and how indigenous African logic, ethics and institutions affect the flow of people, goods, services, resources, ideas and knowledge within the city, as well as what role these factors play in a metropolitan lifestyle that seems to be based on frugalism and inclusion. The survey also sought to understand how social bonds between the traders affect learning and mentoring processes, forms of governance and the management of surplus production and exchange.

In the course of my research, I conducted interviews with Charles Rubia, Nairobi's first African mayor, and Gitu Wa Kahengeri, secretary-general of the Mau Mau War Veterans Association. I also interviewed six elders who I regard as wise and knowledgeable about African logic, norms and values in business, namely: Ignatius Gacheru, Richard Gitau, Njogu Wanguu, Philomena Njeri Mbari, Deborah Kinuthia and Edith Muhindi.

In terms of theory, I build on Myers' (2011) observation that African cities have unique cultural forms and try to respond to the theoretical debates steered by Roy (2011) on whether subaltern urbanism is possible. My hope is that this study will allow for a deeper understanding of how Nairobi's markets are structured and organised as well as their impact on the city's urbanisation process, and that this will in turn contribute to the discourse on urban planning and economies in African cities.

This book is divided into three parts. In Part 1, which is comprised of three chapters, the focus is on global theories of urban planning, and how these have impacted on the development and history of Nairobi. In Chapter 2, I consider how global economic thinking has impacted on Kenya since 1900. In Chapter 3, I provide a brief history of urban planning in Nairobi. In Chapter 4, I review some of the literature on urban theory and its application to African cities and outline my own view of how economic informality and the work of traders and artisans shape urban spaces. To do this, I attempt to uncover the logic of their business practices, norms and values, to show how these derive from traditional norms and values.

In Part 2, which encompasses Chapters 5 and 6, the spotlight falls on the indigenisation or Africanisation of Nairobi, with particular emphasis on the city's markets and how they have created what I call the African metropolis.

Part 3 focuses on utu-ubuntu and the role it plays in urban resilience. Accordingly, in Chapter 7, I describe the utu-ubuntu business model, its basic values and practices. In Chapter 8, I outline the relationships, networks and associations that traders and artisans establish to support one another. I show how they draw on African tradition and allocate their surplus income to shape urban space in ways that work for them. In Chapter 9, I describe some of the methods of self- and group regulation that traders use to ensure the smooth running of their communities. In the final chapter, I discuss possible ways of broadening and formalising the utu-ubuntu model in urban practice through the establishment of what I call cultural villages.

Part One

Traders, Artisans and Urban Planning

Chapter 2

Traders and artisans in global economic thinking

African traders and artisans exist in an environment that is subject to global economic thinking. Their agency in maintaining their identity as traders and craftspeople amid the wave of globalisation and neoliberal thinking is intriguing. Africa has been subjected to modernisation, dependency, market fundamentalism, the digital revolution, the ethics of Confucianism and global entrepreneurship in various attempts to make it work in tandem with the great transformation of the world's economies.

Africa's endeavours to keep up with high-income regions such as Europe, North America and, more recently, East Asia have involved adopting foreign economic systems. In this process, African cultural logic and economic norms have been repressed, as have the roles played by key actors, including traders and artisans. As Mkandawire (2014) observes, despite Africa's struggle to implement the West's economic doctrines for decades, the continent still lags behind in terms of social, political and economic development. In this chapter, I consider how African business logic and economic actors have interacted with global economic thinking, including modernisation and market fundamentalism. I show that they have not only survived repression but have also become what Mkandawire describes as a source of 'uncreative destruction'.

For reasons of space, I will not comprehensively trace Africa's encounters with global economic systems, but simply note that glaring manifestations of these remain. Islamic influence remains evident in Swahili culture along the east coast. Portuguese influence in Kenya is clear at Fort Jesus, and Western colonial influence is generally evident in the widespread adoption of Christianity, industrialisation and urbanisation. A trajectory can be drawn from when Africa's business logic and norms and actors were considered primitive and backward to the continent's current position as a 'final frontier' for economic expansionism. This trajectory can be divided into four eras: the colonial period, the postcolonial period, the neoliberal era, and the contemporary era of increasing Chinese and East Asian influence alongside the strong entrepreneurship lobby led by Barack Obama's Global Entrepreneurship Summit (GES), which is backed by various donors and multinational corporations.

The colonial period

The Berlin Conference of 1884 and 1885 formalised Western colonial territories in Africa. The African continent was carved up into nation-states and these were shared out between the British, French, Portuguese, Germans and Belgians. Under this arrangement, King (1990) observes, Africa became a producer and exporter of raw materials, such as minerals, cotton, palm oil, wheat, wood and sugar cane to the metropole or the world market. In other words, the carving out of these countries involved the introduction of Western capitalism and urbanisation. Taxation of the local populations ensured that many had to leave their farms and villages to seek work in mines or building roads and railways, while local peasant producers were recruited into producing food for workers in the mining enclaves and ports. Gradually, Africa was drawn into supplying the colonial economies with raw materials and buying back manufactured goods. This international divide remains largely unchanged. Africa still exports its raw materials, including minerals, oil, coffee, tea and cotton, to the North. Along with several other scholars, Collier (2010) has described Africa's bountiful natural wealth as 'a resource curse'. Africa's resources have made it all too easy for multinational corporations to convince African leaders to export raw materials in ways that enrich the elite and leave the majority of citizens impoverished and excluded, even though this has created major conflicts at times.

Colonialism also had a strong bearing on the spatial positioning and planning of cities on the continent (King 1990). The first urban settlements that emerged were port cities – points from which raw materials could be exported and imported, and manufactured goods could be dispatched inland. Inland settlements – Nairobi, Kinshasa, Kigali, Kampala, Bujumbura, and so on – served primarily as centres of administration and control. Many of these survive as the capital cities of various African countries. These cities were often the site of difficult encounters between Western and African economic logic, values and norms; this was where the capitalist and pre-capitalist systems confronted one another (see King 1990).

For most of the colonial period, African business logic, norms and values were portrayed by the colonisers as primitive and backward. This convenient delusion put Africa on the receiving end of supposedly well-meaning attempts to bring about modernisation. To this end, Western education systems and Christianity were imposed alongside Western capitalism.

With visions of 'civilising' and modernising African culture, the French and the Portuguese colonial authorities initiated assimilation processes whereby individuals who met certain criteria were selected for education in France and Portugal before being returned home to administer colonial rule. Under the British, missionaries introduced modernisation and Western education to the colonies.

In Kenya, which was colonised by Britain, individuals who sought a British education and adopted its culture were considered modern and were referred to locally as *athomi* (the literate). As recently as 1945, the *Report of the Commission on Higher Education in the Colonies* (also known as the Asquith Report) recommended that higher education in the British colonies be tailored to producing African graduates with just enough skills to serve and preserve the colonial system, rather than skilled thinkers who would creatively address the challenges facing their countries. Graduates were given jobs in government service as clerks, teachers, nurses and secretaries; many migrated to the cities and towns in Kenya to serve in these new roles. The *athomi* soon constituted a new elite and, after Kenya won its independence in 1963, they assumed the status of the ruling elite.

Many scholars have noted that colonialism served to 'under-develop' African countries. For example, Van Zwanenberg and King (1975) observe that, besides plundering and exporting their mineral wealth, the colonial authorities allocated the most fertile lands to European settlers and encouraged settlers to take on entrepreneurial roles, while imposing taxes on the African populations and leaving them with few options other than to become migrant labourers. A host of laws and regulations barred Africans from participating in trade. The sale of livestock, for example, was strictly controlled through quarantine laws that specifically excluded pastoralists. African farming communities were forbidden to grow cash crops and prevented from getting their produce to markets. In many instances, Africans were denied land, and herded into reserves where even subsistence farming was challenging (Van Zwanenberg & King 1975).

Today, migration patterns are such that most of the young people in rural areas migrate into cities and towns. Those who have passed the national school-leaving examinations seek employment in government, multinational corporations, NGOs, international development agencies such as the UN and the World Bank, or in domestic firms involved in banking, as well as in the service industries. Those who do less well at school are employed as security, cleaning, driving or factory workers. Scott (2011) refers to this latter category of workers as 'servile', while Standing (2011) labels them the 'precariat'. Those who do not fit into either of these two categories tend to become traders and artisans, carving out a space for themselves in the informal sector.[1]

Perhaps colonialism's greatest blow to Africa was the decimation of its arts and crafts, which constituted its traditional manufacturing base. In 1949, the German missionary and linguist DiedrichWestermann noted that he could not foresee a time when 'Negro Africa' would be a manufacturing centre. This statement still holds true. Africa has yet to become a manufacturing power.

Westermann (1949: 38) also observed that some forms of art and craft persist, noting that

> In some communities some specialised groups of individual craftsmen emerge. Individual craftsmen [*sic*] spring up, or social groups engage in some special craft with the result that a tribal caste or local industry develops. These are conditioned not only by natural gift inclination but also by the occurrence of suitable materials such as certain plants, clay, iron, salt, which are exploited by a group and the finished articles traded to neighbours. Such tribal or group crafts are, for example in West Africa those of the smith, goldsmith, weaver, potter, wood-worker, leather dresser, rope maker, boat builder, and also the trader.

Westermann went on to say that European penetration destroyed the foundations on which these artistic and manufacturing processes had been built. Art and creativity flourishes best in stable and secure conditions. Under colonialism, peace of mind was vanquished as the colonisers set new tasks and directives. The schooling system destroyed the careful and meticulous apprenticeships that children had served under their elders. Chiefs who had previously invited artists to visit their homesteads to practise and share their skills had to spend their energies collecting taxes or fighting off tax collectors, while still presiding over community disputes and grooming successors.

Certainly, the introduction of European tools and technologies contributed to the demise of many African crafts and industries. Those that have survived in Kenya, such as Kisii soapstone, beadwork, basket weaving and blacksmithing, for example, have survived despite being undermined by the schooling system and crowded out by imported goods.

Postcolonial conundrums

From the early 1960s, a new sense of hope pervaded many African countries, as country after country achieved independence. It did not take long for hopes to be dashed as Africa's place at the bottom of the world economic pecking order remained set in stone and new ruling elites rushed to emulate their colonial rulers in accumulating extravagant wealth, facilitating widespread corruption and failing to provide the most basic of services to their people.

Several theories have been put forward to explain Africa's lack of progress. I touch briefly on just two: the modernisation paradigm which was first to emerge in the early 1960s, and the dependency model which dominated debates in the 1970s and 1980s.

The modernisation paradigm was largely informed by the work of Hoselitz (1952), McClelland (1961) and Hagen (1963), who attributed the lack of development and advancement in Africa to traditional values relating to family and kinship. According to McClelland, for example, the absence of entrepreneurship in Africa is attributable to individuals' lack of ambition and low orientation towards achievement. Hagen observes that family members are locked and boxed into routine patterns that hinder their creativity. From this perspective, modernisation requires creative individuals to break away from traditional values and create business elites that are capable of steering capitalist development in Africa (see Leys 1994). This paradigm does not see traditional values as contributing anything positive to development but rather as a set of attitudes awaiting transformation through modernisation. Viewed through this lens, African markets offer nothing more than a way station or a set of stopgap measures while communities await 'true' modernisation and development. Those who cling to this paradigm, and there are many who do, focus on entrepreneurial training, foreign investment, and the expansion of education as solutions to Africa's social and economic problems.

By contrast, Latin American theorist Gunder Frank (1966) argued that the reason for underdevelopment in postcolonial states is their economic dependence on Europe and North America. Writers such as Walter Rodney (1972) demonstrated how Europe underdeveloped African countries for centuries by expropriating their land and mineral resources and exploiting their labour, while sending their own poverty (that is, their poorer citizens) to the colonies. The dependency perspective holds that development will be impossible until African countries transform their relationships with the developed world, reclaim their power in terms of trade relations and receive reparations for the losses they have suffered. This perspective also views the wealthy elites that exist in low-income countries as a *comprador* class or agents of international capital (Leys 1994).

Frantz Fanon famously described Africans as the 'wretched of the earth' (Fanon 1963). Viewed through this lens, African traders and artisans might be seen as having little choice but to wait for or join a revolution. Whether the wretched of the earth can be expected to lead revolutions has since been questioned by several scholars. Spivak (1988), for example, suggests that subalterns are silenced by their dual domination by local and international elites. However, other scholars propose that all peasants are basically revolutionaries. Guha (1999) and Jazeel (2014) argue that people in poor communities have a complex dialectical relationship with geopolitical hegemony, and that they use their knowledge of this to further their own interests and subvert the dominant system in subtle and complex ways.

In my view, the survival and persistence of Africa's traders and artisans, who establish and run markets in cities where formal businesses are privileged in many ways, parallels the peasant insurgency that Guha describes. In Kenya's markets, traders and artisans engage in business largely autonomously and control certain aspects of trade and manufacturing in the city in mostly non-violent ways. The artisans continually create, copy and reverse-engineer new products. Traders pool their savings, share space, provide security and surety for one another and reduce their transaction costs through forms of entrepreneurialism based on solidarity (Kinyanjui 2014). They also pool their skills and experiences and set their own rules and regulations.

The neoliberal era

In the late 1980s and early 1990s, both the World Bank and the International Monetary Fund (IMF) introduced market fundamentalism to Africa via enforced structural adjustment programmes. The apparent purpose of these programmes was to revive and entrench capitalism in African economies that had been adversely affected by the oil crises of the 1970s and the decline in commodity prices. According to the IMF, Africa's economies were being eroded by governments spending too much on welfare and on subsidising certain sectors of the economy by funding parastatal organisations. In their view, state intervention needed to be rolled back so that the 'free' market would be able to direct the flow of goods and services, stimulating economic growth.

In effect, the World Bank and the IMF attached conditions to their loans such that state subsidies had to be withdrawn from sectors such as primary education and health and many civil servants were retrenched to enable governments to cut their wage bills. In Kenya, cooperatives were restructured and encouraged to become private entities. Cost sharing was introduced in schools and hospitals. The state withdrew its investments in parastatals, such as the Industrial and Commercial Development Corporation, Kenya Railways and the Kenya National Trading Corporation, and undertook to play only a supervisory role. At the same time, bank interest rates were freed and the removal of exchange controls meant that import duties and protection for nascent industries were done away with. In line with these measures, the Nairobi City Commission stopped constructing housing for low-income groups – their expectation being that market forces would step in instead.

In 1986, the Kenyan government drafted Sessional Paper No. 1: Economic Management for Renewed Growth and Management. Unlike in Sessional Paper No. 10 of 1965, basic human norms and the values of African socialism are not mentioned. The market is presented as a substitute for social and economic policy. The independence and self-reliance envisaged in 1965 were curtailed as local industries were closed and foreign goods began to be imported.

The end of the cooperative movement and state welfarism was tantamount to the killing of African socialism. Structural adjustment was about promoting individualism through entrepreneurialism and resource allocation through market forces and taxation. At this point, community mobilisation and participation in the harambee movement (via which individuals made contributions to development projects in their own areas) was abolished and replaced by the Constituency Development Fund.

While the government deployed the tools of structural adjustment to restructure Kenya's formal economy, traders and artisans in African markets were not cushioned from its effects in any way. Instead, they were left to their own devices to face the changes introduced by the removal of exchange controls and the flood of cheap foreign goods into the Kenyan market.

Traders, artisans and others who were excluded from the new system turned to their past in search of support (Kinyanjui 2012). African markets became safe havens for people who had been excluded from the formal economy. As Bangura (1994) observes, middle-class people in Nigeria who were adversely affected by structural adjustment also moved into economic informality at this time. This heightened activities in African markets, making them very crowded.

The new millennium, the digital revolution and the impact of China and East Asia

In some quarters, the digital revolution is viewed as a magic wand that will help Africa catch up with the rest of the world and finally achieve the great transformation. For this reason, many countries have invested heavily in digital infrastructure and encouraged private investors to follow suit. It is certainly true that traders and artisans use mobile telephony extensively to transfer money, place orders, provide customer service, and so on. However, while technology has enhanced the face-to-face transactions and the solidarity that exists between traders and artisans, this is arguably still more attributable to their existing social networks, which are firmly based on bonds of kinship, friendship and ethnicity.

Certainly, many traders and artisans are internet savvy. They have email and some use their own websites as well as platforms such as Facebook, WhatsApp and Instagram to market their goods and services or to communicate with others. However, the application of digital technology in artisanal production and processing is still limited and most of this is still done manually. The adoption and application of digital technologies in production needs to be given serious thought. The potential for a digital revolution in areas such as computer-aided designs, laser cutting of materials, as well as in knitting, embroidery, stitching, carving, folding, welding, and so on is yet to be realised. However, part of the appeal of handmade items is that they require skill and dexterity rather than relying on expensive machinery and/or software that has to be imported and requires specialist knowledge or expensive parts to maintain and repair.

Since the mid-2000s, China's forays into Kenya have been made mainly via universities and government departments. The focus seems to be on winning the support of Kenya's elite, so Kenya's leaders have trooped off to China while the Chinese reciprocate by visiting Kenya and there is a lot of talk about friendship and win-win relationships. China's policy on international development is geared towards the construction of infrastructure, including sea and airports that service special economic zones, as well as highways and superhighways. The aim seems to be to open Africa up to further globalisation and liberalisation but also to allow for the more efficient export of raw materials to China to feed its growing manufacturing sector.

Kenya's Vision 2030 follows the Chinese model in its focus on the development of infrastructure and special economic zones. Several Kenyan universities have established Confucius Institutes. The intention seems to be to capture the future elite, expose them to Chinese culture and language, and persuade them to accept Chinese influence. However, if African identity and philosophy are submerged in this process, this may pave the way for control and exploitation by China in the long term.

The Kenyan government has already lost touch with ordinary Kenyans on the question of China's role and influence. Unlike the government, traders and artisans in Nairobi have demonstrated against Chinese infiltration into small enterprises and hawking. Contemporary popular culture and music highlights resistance to the Kenyan government's get-rich-quick approach to relations with China. In his song *Mbara ya Mukimo*,[2] Magua Kio narrates the experience of someone who sells soil to the Chinese, squanders the proceeds and is left a pauper. The song is an appeal to Kenyan government officials and business leaders to rethink the long-term impact of their economic partnerships, paradigms and deals. While the dominant global economic paradigms cannot be wished away, Africa needs a purposefully differentiated and integrated economic approach that accommodates both foreign models and African values. A creative synergy between Western and Oriental capitalism and Africa's indigenous economic systems needs to be developed to produce a unique and viable economic model for the African continent.

As the former governor of the Central Bank of Nigeria, Sanusi Lamido Sanusi, observes, 'neither the Washington Consensus nor the Beijing Consensus can bring about the desired change. The implications of the structure of African economies need to be critically appraised in order to identify an appropriate African Consensus for its development model' (Sanusi 2012).

The 2009 Global Entrepreneurship Summit (GES)

In a post on the Nordic Africa Institute's blog entitled 'The economy of affection important as ever in Tanzania', the influential Norwegian academic Goran Hydén (2014) observes that economic informality constitutes the rubric of the uncaptured peasantry in Africa. Kenya's informal sector was not captured by the state in the 1960s and 1970s or by the free-market fundamentalism of the 1980s and 1990s. It will therefore be interesting to observe whether or not Barack Obama's GES initiative will capture Africa's traders and artisans and propel Africa through some form of great transformation.

When Obama started his first term as US president in 2009, he was very aware of the effects of the global economic crisis that began in 2008. Soon after taking office, Obama initiated the first of a series of GES to create a new way for the US to engage aspects of the world's economies over which it could not yet claim to hold sway. Accordingly, the GES promotes entrepreneurship as a means of forging partnerships between America and the rest of the world. Touted as an alternative to military engagement, they have so far been run with the aim of reducing global tension and spurring productivity, and have been held in various parts of the world. The first was in the US (2009), followed by Egypt (2010), Turkey (2011), Morocco (2012), the United Arab Emirates (2013), Malaysia (2014), Kenya (2015), the US (2016) and India (2017). Summit participants are drawn from all over the world, and include entrepreneurs, investors, academics, non-profit organisations, foundations and businesses.

The GES operates on the assumption that entrepreneurship is the foundation of wealth, and that wealth is a harbinger of peace and harmony as well as an antidote to violence, extremism and corruption. Entrepreneurship is therefore seen as a panacea for the issues of job creation, youth empowerment and the efficient delivery of basic services such as health and education. Apparently, wealth helps citizens stand up for their rights and push back corruption, erodes barriers between communities and cultures and builds bridges that help people address shared problems. Entrepreneurship is therefore promoted as having the potential to solve the world's social and economic problems by tapping into humanity's infinite imaginative and creative powers.

Goals of global entrepreneurship engagement

In my opinion, the goals of the US-led global entrepreneurship movement are twofold. The first is to help revive the global economy by opening up new markets to existing capitalist enterprises by encouraging them to 'build partnerships'. The second is to transform 'non-capitalist economies', especially those in Africa so that they conform to the Western view of what an economy is. This scenario differs little from the colonial template imposed in the 19th century or the neoliberal one that replaced it.

The rationale behind the GES lies in the fact that the world is now more interconnected than ever. Finally recognising that an action in one part of the world affects the rest of the world, the US is trying to get countries to work together. As Obama noted at the 2009 GES forum in Washington:

> We are all bound together by certain common aspirations – to live in dignity, to get an education, to live healthy lives and, maybe, start a business without having to pay tribute or a bribe to anyone, to speak freely and have a say in how we are governed, to live in peace and security and to give our children a better future. (Biden 2011)

Joe Biden echoed this in a slightly more revealing statement at the 2011 GES forum in Istanbul:

> When a financial system weakens in one country, prosperity is hurt everywhere. When a new flu infects one human being, all are at risk. When one nation pursues a nuclear weapon, the risk of nuclear attack rises for all nations. When violent extremists operate in one stretch of mountains, people are endangered across an ocean. (Biden 2011)

While the ideals and aspirations of dignity, freedom, peace, health, education and work are laudable, to understand the role and potential impact of the GES, it must be viewed through the lenses of colonialism and structural adjustment that have previously attempted to shape Africa's economies in the interests of global trade. Table 2 provides a simplistic representation of three phases of capitalist development in Africa. These are comparable to the three waves of capitalism experienced in the Western world as outlined by Scott and Storper (1986).

For centuries, Africa has been bombarded by global economic agendas that have been developed and imposed without its representation. In general, the implementation of these agendas has been inconsistent and the outcomes dismal. Their failure is reflected in the presence of huge slums and the fact that traders and artisans, who have largely been excluded from these agendas, continue to play a major part in helping millions of Africans to secure a livelihood for themselves. In other words, despite having been key players in African economies for centuries, traders and artisans have been entirely unrepresented in the formulation and implementation of global economic development paradigms.

TABLE *2 Aspects of capitalist development imposed on Africa*

Features	Colonialism	Neoliberalism	Global entrepreneurship
Ideology	Enrich Europe and bring light to the 'dark continent' through Christianity and modernisation	Entrench capitalism and democracy through liberalising trade and encourage the 'global free market'	Entrench capitalism through globalisation Individual rights must be respected
Target	All Africans Focus on men	All Africans	Focus on youth and women
Methodology	Military occupation Settlement, exploitation and taxation Open schools and mission stations Punish people who practise indigenous traditions	Provide aid and attach conditions Impose structural adjustment programmes and collect interest on debt Privatise state institutions Open the economy to foreign competition Undermine indigenous traditions Offer scholarships to encourage brain drain	Continue to collect debt and interest on debt Roll back the state and reduce democratic participation to voting Talk about partnerships but never discuss power imbalances Crush dissension Turn global entrepreneurs into celebrities Foster corruption Exploit indigenous traditions for profit Offer mentorships and coaching
Actors/agents	Military forces Colonial administrators Missionaries Settlers	World Bank IMF Donor organisations Multinational corporations and their marketing agencies NGOs	Global industrialists and funders NGOs Governments pretending to be democracies Deep state
Outcomes	Enclave development Inequality between men and women Death of tradition Creation of nation states Introduction of Western ideology and Christian belief	Rising inequality with the majority living in poverty Free trade kills local manufacturing Neo-traditionalism and economic informality emerge Rise of violent fundamentalists	Entrenched poverty and inequality Large-scale migrations Western enclaves protected by private security firms Society fracturing along lines of class, age and gender Growing resistance to Westernisation

The GES is a case in point. It assumes an entrepreneurship *tabula rasa* in Africa and proposes a whole range of training programmes which completely overlooks the fact that generations of entrepreneurs have been systematically nurtured and mentored in the face of a host of discriminatory and repressive measures imposed by city authorities. In the next chapter, I outline the history of discrimination and repression that traders and artisans in Nairobi have encountered and resisted.

Chapter 3

Urban planning and economic informality in Nairobi: A brief history

Urban planning is the art and science of ensuring regulation and order in cities. It involves managing human interactions with and within the physical and built environment. While planning has been relatively successful in many European and North American cities, similar success has been elusive in Africa, Latin America and parts of Asia, where the prevalence of slums and economic informality has a massive impact.

In this chapter, I trace the origin of economic informality in Nairobi and city planners' efforts to address this during the colonial, postcolonial and neoliberal periods. This review reveals the extent to which planners are affected by dominant economic models. It also shows how, in all three periods, urban planning has tended to isolate and marginalise, rather than accommodate, traders and artisans.

Planning during the colonial era

Colonial administrators never intended Africans to be real players in global cities. Rather than ever owning the means of production and exchange, their lot was to work in mines or on plantations around the urban areas, or temporarily provide labour in warehouses, homes and shops in the city. Africans were seen as itinerant residents who would eventually return to their ancestral homes in the rural areas (Mbiti 1969). To a limited extent, Africans who adopted aspects of Western culture and religion after undergoing colonial and missionary education were made more welcome in the urban settlements. Traders and artisans, who tended to have limited access to formal education, faced several obstacles in their bid to gain entry into the city.

The Local Government Municipalities Ordinance of 1928 was the Colony and Protectorate of Kenya's first attempt to initiate urban planning. The ordinance defined a municipality as an 'area or district placed under the jurisdiction of a municipal council or municipal board' (Colony and Protectorate of Kenya 1928). For Nairobi, which was not an established settlement prior to British occupation and which grew around a railway depot built in 1899, the ordinance provided a framework for managing the municipality and for incorporating Africans into the emerging urban economy. Issues such as the constitution of the city council, property ownership in relation to housing and industrial sites, the occupation and licensing of premises, street trading, native passes, native labour and the layout of so-called native locations were addressed. In addition, offensive trades, food and drink, peddlers and hawkers, and markets were regulated.

Of course, the ordinance was in no way representative of the interests of the native inhabitants of the city, and local Kenyans were denied the right to representation in municipal planning from the outset. No Africans were appointed to the municipal council. Instead, it comprised of nine elected Europeans, seven Indian members nominated by the governor, two additional members nominated by the governor and one administrative officer who was charged with safeguarding native interests (Colony and Protectorate of Kenya 1928).

The ordinance empowered the council to designate and control places for Africans. It mandated the council to erect suitable buildings and ensure that natives lived in the locations delineated for them. Only domestic workers who lodged on the premises of their employers or received exemption from the governor could reside outside of these locations (Colony and Protectorate of Kenya 1928: 75). Other regulatory aspects included the supervising and inspecting of the native location, the issuing of passes and ensuring that native Kenyans carried these. The ordinance also controlled natives' access to the streets and the licensing of native labour.

In addition, the council was mandated to regulate trade licences, the occupation of premises, and to appoint a committee to review applications for trade licences (Colony and Protectorate of Kenya 1928: 117). Accordingly, the ordinance defined where public markets could be situated, and the council was mandated to establish and regulate markets, set dues and prohibit the establishment of any markets that did not have all the necessary permissions from the council (Colony and Protectorate of Kenya 1928: 107).

To sum up, the ordinance controlled the movement of native Africans in the city, restricted them to living and working in particular spaces and regulated their access to the economy via the use of licenses and dues. Effectively, the ordinance denied Africans any claim to urban citizenship and it established control over markets in ways that ran contrary to the spirit of African indigenous markets, which traditionally were open to all. After 1928, all African traders and artisans were classified as 'hawkers'. Bylaw 325 of the ordinance defines a hawker as 'any person who whether as principal, agent, or employee carries on the business of offering or exposing goods for sale, barter or exchange, elsewhere than at a fixed place'. Significantly, this bylaw has since been reinstated numerous times, with few changes.

By the 1930s, African traders and artisans were already in conflict with Nairobi's city council over taxes and space. Taxes introduced by the ordinance were alien to indigenous trade practices. According to archival records, by 1936, Akamba handcraft traders were burdened with such heavy taxes that the district commissioner asked the town clerk to determine whether they could be exempted from paying the monthly 20-shilling tax.[3] A Mr SM Fichat was also troubled by the lack of space available for Akamba hawkers and asked the district commissioner to reserve space at the railway station 'where the boys can sell their wares to passengers'.[4] Meanwhile, the plight of other African hawkers in the city is captured in a letter written by tea vendors to the town clerk, which reads as follows:

The Town Clerk
Municipal Council of Nairobi

Copy to His Worship the Mayor

We the undersigned tea sellers beg to most humbly and respectfully write you the following request: We have been informed that you determine to abolish our insignificant trading. Therefore we take the liberty of writing and ask you whether you have pity upon us, we miserable sellers; for we have not money enough to hire a little local hotel in town and carry our business there, then it is more difficult to move at our special places and push our selling carts about the Nairobi streets where there are much dust and we are afraid that our customers will not accept to drink our dusty tea; it is grievance to us when the completeness of your consideration will be to end on the matter therefore we take the liberty of asking you to accept and let us go on with our work as well as we are doing.

We trust you will consider the above application and your kind consideration.

We have the honour to be Sir,

Njoroge wa Mwara, Nganga wa Karanja, Nganga wa Kimani, Wacama Kanyororo, Ngugi Waringui, Nganga wa Rurigi, Mukua wa Kimani, Kariuki wa Gachoka, Gathuni wa Mutuambuni, Ngari wa Hika.[5]

Meanwhile, African traders faced ongoing battles related to lack of capital, poor infrastructure, the demolition of their structures and opposition from Asian and European businessmen. For example, a Mr W Evans, general secretary of the East African Traders Association, argued that hawkers were 'detrimental to ordinary legitimate trading'.[6] The Indian Christian Union complained that native banana and snuff sellers were 'a nuisance' for squatting near the Indian club fence and for turning the space into a native market; they petitioned the town clerk to remove the natives from the area.[7]

In later years, various revisions and amendments were made to the Local Government Municipalities Ordinance of 1928. In 1937, it was amended to incorporate the words 'native handicrafts'. In 1942, amendments Bylaw 325 of the 1928 ordinance was amended after the council received complaints about traders, and trading fees were revised in an attempt to further control and regulate 'hawkers' in the city. Several categories of fees were introduced at this time. Thus, selling flowers attracted an annual fee of 30 shillings in scheduled areas. Selling charcoal or newspapers in any part of the city attracted a fee of 1 shilling per month or 10 shillings per year. Selling vegetables, fruits, and other farm produce cost 1 shilling per month or 10 shillings per year. To receive a general licence to hawk in any part of the municipality or within scheduled areas, a trader had to pay 20 shillings per month or 200 shillings per annum. For ease of identification and to differentiate them from 'loafers and idlers', traders also had to purchase and carry badges at a cost of 2 shillings each. This was another way for the council to control the number of hawkers in the city.

Further amendments to Bylaw 325 were adopted in 1942 to redefine areas in the city in which hawking was permitted. These were delineated by the railway crossing at Kingsway; the area to the northwest of Kingsway and the Government Road (now Moi Avenue) junction; the area southeast and northeast of the junction between Government Road and Fort Hall Road (now Muranga Road); the western and northwestern boundaries of Fort Hall Road to Nairobi River and downstream to Racecourse Road; south of White House Road (now Parliament Road); and northwest of the railway line.

Established shopkeepers strongly opposed these amendments. For example, the East African Traders Association objected on the grounds that the amendments would be detrimental to shopkeepers in the commercial area and argued that as shopkeepers they were entitled to protection because they paid licences and fees. It was also alleged that hawkers obtained licences to cloak nefarious activities such as petty and large theft. On the other hand, the editor of the *Sunday Post* opposed the fee introduced for newspaper vendors, arguing not only that it was too expensive, but that on Sundays vendors worked half days and thus would not be able to raise the required fee. However, the editor then recommended that the number of badges issued to vendors be reduced to control competition.[8]

From this point on, free entry into any trade or craft in the city was closed off. A licence and a defined business space were made compulsory. In this way, the urban economy was contested by informal African traders and artisans on the one hand, and white or Indian traders on the other. In time, this became a source of conflict that prevented the development of relationships between these sets of traders and created a divide that still prevails.[9]

The 1950s were tumultuous for the colony as Kenyans began clamouring for more space and opportunity. In the hope of maintaining their hold over the country, the colonial authorities initiated reforms to create more latitude for African participation.[10] Accordingly, they passed the African District Council Ordinance of 1950 to introduce palliative measures that they hoped would manage the rising agitation of the Kenyan people. The African district council was given the powers to license traders and deal with trade disputes. The ordinance covered the establishment, regulation and construction of markets as well as the letting out of market stands and the setting of fees for licences and permits. Licensing was not scrapped as traders had hoped, as it was considered crucial for the maintenance of health, safety, well-being, good governance and as a revenue stream for the municipality.

As per the 1950 ordinance, African district councils were established to represent African interests and to serve as courts for cases in which Africans were tried. The African district council was given the authority to introduce bylaws in respect of matters such as:

- Prohibiting, regulating or controlling trade outside of established markets;
- Inspecting, supervising and licensing of social halls and places of entertainment, as well as lodging and eating houses;
- Controlling, supervising and licensing of millers, barbers, hide and skin traders, butchers, carpenters, blacksmiths, shoemakers, tailors, musicians, bicycle and vehicle mechanics, stationers, weavers and spinners, painters, bakers, charcoal burners, firewood dealers, confectioners, quarries and brick-making yards; nursery stores, the hiring of canoes and ploughs, hotels and restaurants and slaughter houses, among other professions.

Africans were appointed as representatives on these councils and soon helped to encourage more African participation in trade. A small number of Africans were licensed to trade in beer, charcoal, general shops and the transport business. However, hawking and artisanal work were unaffected by this as the ordinance differentiated trade from hawking. In essence, the 1950 ordinance created the basis for a dual economy, and quickly led to the emergence of a small African elite. Africans who could afford to join the formal economy were managed and regulated by the African district council while the formal European economy remained under the control of the national government. Traders and artisans were still regulated via a separate hawking bylaw and remained excluded from the formal economy.

By 1962, a hawkers' licence issued under a new bylaw defined trade as 'the sale or exposure of goods for sale in a shop for the purpose of profit' and defined a shop as 'any building or part thereof or any place whether or not such a place was a building'.[11] Under the same bylaw, only individuals could be licensed as hawkers. This represented a major blow to the traditional African way of life. It encouraged individuals to be solo entrepreneurs instead of allowing them to include relatives and friends in their ventures as tradition and good business practice dictated. Nevertheless, traders and artisans quickly formed associations to provide the synergies they needed to carry out business in the city. These associations also served as platforms for lobbying the council. Examples of these associations include the Nairobi Kimathi Market Society, the Kenya Street Traders' Society and the Vegetable and Fruit Hawkers' Association.

Planning in the postcolonial era

Nairobi's transformation from a colonial to a postcolonial city has not been easy. Four main epochs are evident so far and are discussed in the sections that follow. They cover the following years: 1963 to 1982; 1983 to 1991; 1992 to 2000; and 2001 to 2010, with each phase informed by wider socio-economic values and discourses. These range from African socialism and communitarian values to individualism, and from market fundamentalism to distributive capitalism. As these different value systems and discourses have struggled to gain ascendancy in the city, dissonances and incongruencies have emerged. These too have left their own spatial imprints and added further diversity to the city's economy and territorial complexity.

Growth and welfare: 1963–1982

The process of transforming Nairobi into a truly African city began with the Africanisation of the administration after independence. Charles Rubia was elected as the city's first African mayor. Among the biggest challenges Rubia had to deal with were the problems affecting the city's African residents who had been confined to the famous African quarter, Eastlands.

This period was characterised by the provision of welfare and urban growth in line with the values of African socialism and communitarianism. This was propped up, to some extent, by Europe and the US offering aid to former colonies in an effort to win allies during the Cold War. The city's main objective was to address the social problems that affected most citizens, including poverty and poor education.[12]

Quoted in the *Daily Nation* newspaper on 27 July 1965, Rubia said he was alarmed by the increasing number of beggars on the streets, most of whom were women. He noted that when he had become mayor in 1962, about 250 beggars lived in Nairobi and that this number had since increased tremendously. He stated that he was also 'shocked and dispirited' to see the growing number of cripples on the streets and believed that they could be useful citizens. To address these problems, Rubia asked the government to provide K£5 000[13] to transform Forest Inn on Kiambu Road into a rehabilitation centre where beggars could learn craft and farming skills. The city's aim seems to have been to offer an inclusive welfare policy for all residents.

Financing and forward planning in terms of rates collection, local governance and education were key issues during this period. In a memorandum to a commission headed by WS Hardacre, a British local government expert, Rubia expressed concern about the need to increase rates revenue for the city authorities from K£1.3 million to K£3.4 million by 1970,[14] and about the city being involved in running secondary schools.

Rubia's policies on education were characteristic of his tenure. He saw education as integral to urbanisation and to Kenya's overall development. Consequently, he encouraged racial integration in schools and funded the growth of educational institutions. Rubia reportedly observed: 'We firmly believe that only the best in primary education is good enough for Nairobi.'[15] To achieve this, he proposed that the budget for primary education be increased from K£780 000 to K£1 million. New schools were opened in Kariobangi, Kileleshwa, Ofafa, Westlands, Makongeni, Garden Estate, Dagoretti and Riruta. In addition, in 1964, schools such as Nairobi South Primary enrolled their first cohort of African pupils.

Slum clearance was another major policy goal during Rubia's tenure as mayor. Providing decent housing was seen as a symbol of winning the war against poverty, and it was hoped that well-designed accommodation would promote health and inspire self-respect. At the opening of Kariokor Estate in 1966, President Jomo Kenyatta emphasised the importance of providing every family with shelter.[16]

Around this time, the city council funded the development of

Uhuru Estate, which was designed and built entirely by Africans. According to a *Daily Nation* reporter, its completion in 1967 was seen as the fulfilment of the new government's dream of independence.[17] When the Kenya African National Union (KANU) swept to power in 1963, led by Kenyatta, the party's great dream had been to promote the welfare of people whose interests had previously been neglected. The completion of Uhuru Estate was a great step towards the fulfilment of this dream. The estate, consisting of 324 housing units, was used to settle residents who had been living in two-roomed houses in Eastleigh. Another housing programme initiated in this period was the site-and-service scheme at Kariobangi. The scheme began with the construction of a K£ 390 demonstration 'show house' which, according to the mayor, 'anyone could build'. The site-and-service scheme was promoted as being in the spirit of African socialism.[18] Also in this period, the city council obtained Commonwealth funding to develop Woodley-Kibera and Uhuru estates. The Woodley houses were ready for occupation by 1969. Commenting on the development, then national minister for local government, Paul Ngei, stressed that 'health is the main contributing factor to wealth and happiness' and that 'to be healthy, we must live in good houses'.[19]

Issuing hawkers with licences and building a wholesale market

From the mid-1960s, the city council also began searching for a strategy that would accommodate African traders and artisans. Rubia proposed increasing the number of licensed hawkers by issuing another 320 licences, but the senior police officer in the city, a Mr Dawson, opposed this move. Speaking to a newspaper reporter, Rubia observed that he would be very disappointed if the 'proposal to issue more hawkers licenses is turned down merely because Mr Dawson still insists that we should still not have the extra 320'.[20]

Another strategy explored by the council to encourage more African participation in the city's economy was to shift traders off the roadsides and into markets where they could own stalls; Kimathi Market was one example of this.[21] According to Rubia, the national government was in 'complete accord' with the city council in as far as the necessity of helping Africans establish businesses was concerned. 'To this end, both are dedicated towards opening avenues in the economic field so that the existing racial imbalance is corrected.'[22]

In 1965, construction began on a new wholesale market in Mincing Street. Opened in 1966, as Wakulima Market, the premises boasted tarmac surfacing, and water points with surface drainage, and was surrounded by precast concrete walls. Shelving was built of reinforced concrete and rose to a height of nearly 7.5 metres.[23]

The allocation of space for, and construction of, African markets was a first attempt to incorporate an African mode of production into the city. Other attempts included the construction of shopping centres in areas inhabited mostly by working-class Africans, such as Ofafa, Jericho and Lumumba. Once again, however, few traders were given plots on which to build their stalls and conflict arose between them and the owners of commercial land.[24]

City planning and economic management

While progress was made, planning in the postcolonial city was difficult and problematic. The Africans who took over the management of the city faced fundamental challenges. According to rapporteur's notes from a workshop on the management of large cities in Africa that took place in 1973, Nairobi's town clerk reported that the city council had assigned tasks to planners but provided no policy guidelines on housing.[25] The rapporteur also noted that

> Between 1895 and 1920, the planning of Nairobi was never considered seriously and development was uncontrolled and unguided. Planning efforts were first made in 1926 when some controls on zoning were introduced. This was followed by the drawing of a comprehensive plan in 1948. It laid guidelines for development and earmarked land for residential, industrial and roadwork extension. In 1961, another plan was drawn but was abandoned because independence was just around the corner.

The town clerk thus acknowledged that planning was ad hoc and very little forward planning was being carried out while problems accumulated.

By 1967, the need for comprehensive planning had been acknowledged and was implemented with the aim of addressing four key issues: the housing shortage, the shortage of water, traffic congestion and the rapid spread of shanties. It was proposed that planning considerations aim to maximise job growth and attract modern non-agricultural employers, while also promoting the informal sector in ways that would complement the formal sector. Building standards applicable in residential estates were decided on the basis of resources available to the council and to occupants' abilities to pay for services. Housing developments were to be located close to employment opportunities to minimise public expenditure on transport costs. Caution was to be exercised in relation to the uptake of agricultural land by the city.

However, in the 1970s, Nairobi's city planning was increasingly informed by the notion of it being a primate city; that is, it was already disproportionately larger than any other city in the country and housed about a third of the national population.[26] Accordingly, city planners endeavoured to restrict the influx of additional residents, especially those who were considered unemployable, and the government developed rural development policies that envisaged reducing urbanisation and encouraging people in rural areas to remain where they were.

In practice, the resources spent on controlling the movement of people meant fewer funds and people to meet the needs of those already in Nairobi. The solution to unemployment was envisioned in terms of growing the city's modern formal business sector.[27] Those who were not accommodated in this sector were left to create livelihoods for themselves in whatever ways they could. That is, for a few people, incomes rose and some became prosperous, but for the large majority, incomes had hardly risen by the end of the 20th century.

To remedy this situation, the mayor of Nairobi proposed that planning should be done in ways that would enable citizens to understand both the problems faced by the city and the solutions put forward by the city authorities. Nairobi's early planners acknowledged that an understanding of the need for planning was alien to many residents and that opposition was likely from many quarters. In fact, opposition to urban planning is common in most parts of the world. 'Where planning is an alien concept, there is a danger of it being rejected by a majority of people. Even in countries where planning had been in operation for a long time, there are tendencies of regarding it as a negative exercise and therefore dreaded.'[28]

Planning conflicts were also being experienced, as noted in 1973:

> The city council has functions given to it to perform but we have suffered from a general lack of policy guidelines. Construction of markets for hawkers were said to be too elaborate and some were called white elephants. There is free land in our planning and we have been at loggerheads with some ministries with regard to development control. This is not usually welcome. Any developer would like to do what he likes. We insist on standards laid down, for example, on density of population, road thickness and drainage. In this respect we are unpopular. Considerable pressure is brought to bear but we hide under the law.[29]

Nevertheless, the 1970s can still be considered the heyday of development in post-independence Kenya. Planners and residents were imbued with a spirit of self-governance and the desire to make Nairobi a truly African city. For Nairobi to show its African colours, the participation of Africans in governance and commerce was encouraged and African logic and institutions were expected to permeate throughout the social fabric. It was also a time in which those who had fought for freedom were to be rewarded and the national cake equitably shared. The city authorities were concerned about racial integration, especially in education, but also about slum clearance, the development of new housing and health facilities, water security and the building of essential infrastructure.

The city administration aimed to develop policies that included everyone from beggars to slum dwellers, roadside hawkers, shoe shiners and car washers. Programmes were imbued with a spirit of caring and reciprocity. As mayor, Rubia was particularly concerned about education, health, housing and economic opportunities for Africans. At one point, he even threatened to resign if hawkers were not licensed, and confronted Asian councillors, European bureaucrats and city police officials about their negative attitudes to hawkers.

The neoliberal era: Nairobi under the city commission, 1983–1991

In 1983, a task force was appointed to investigate financial mismanagement and poor service delivery by councillors who were part of the elected city government. The task force recommended that control of the city be shifted away from elected officials and into the hands of a commission, the chairperson and members of which would be appointed by the president. The transition was tumultuous and the nine-and-a-half years during which the commission ruled in the city were characterised by gross mismanagement and poor service delivery.

Analysis of various news sources shows that the commission was a microcosm of all that a civilised community loathes – a monolith of incorrigible brutality, inefficiency, terror, lethargy, corruption, dubious transactions, exploitation, incessant squabbling and intolerance. Service fees were collected for services never rendered, water shortages were a permanent feature of the city, shanty dwellers were violently evicted without notice and whole areas were flattened, potholes made road travel hazardous, traders and artisans were harassed, land meant for public utilities was turned to private use and debts were not collected. The city was in a mess. As reporter Shadrack Amkoye wrote, Nairobi was transformed from a 'city in the sun' into a 'city in dirt'.[30]

The city commission's lack of concern for traders and artisans was reflected in the inhumane ways in which it dealt with shanty dwellers and the frequent demolition of traders' kiosks. In 1990, Njoroge Mungai, then-vice chairperson of KANU for the city of Nairobi, reportedly criticised Fred Gumo, who led the commission, for demolishing kiosks that were sources of livelihoods for ordinary people.[31] The commission's policies against ordinary poor people were also reflected by the demolition of Muoroto Village on 25 May 1990. The callousness with which that demolition was carried out was illustrated by the fact that Gumo paraded members of the commission's security forces who carried out the demolition before the press to counter a report by the provost of St Andrews Church that some kiosk owners had died and others had been injured in the process.[32] When the member of parliament for Kamukuji, Maina Wanjigi, asked the commission to admit that brutality had occurred and to resign, he was called a neo-colonialist and sacked by the government of Daniel Arap Moi. The minister for local government went on to justify the demolition, alleging that Muoroto Village was home to 'a den of thieves'.

This behaviour reflected the arrogance and blindness of the governing elite to the plight of ordinary citizens. The whole scenario had to do with perceptions of the governability of people living in poorer areas by those in positions of political privilege. Where were these people expected to go, what were they expected to do thereafter and why was the city victimising them?

Also during the 1980s, several NGOs were established in Kenya. These promised to improve business productivity in ways that the state was not able to do. Examples include the Kenya Rural Enterprise Program (K-Rep) and Faulu Kenya, which both offer micro financing, and the Kenya Management Assistance Programme (K-Map), which aimed to improve links between small and large firms in Kenya.

Nairobi after 1992

When a new and elected city council took over after the 1992 national and local elections, it inherited a host of problems, including the extreme poverty of many residents. Mayor Steve Mwangi organised a convention under the banner 'The Nairobi We

Want', inviting residents and city authorities to discuss strategies for improving the city. Residents were particularly concerned about poor service delivery. The mayor responded by promising that he and his council would sort this out.[33] This period saw the privatisation of services formerly supplied by the city. At the same time, NGOs such as K-Rep, K-Map and Faulu Kenya assumed key roles, delivering welfare services and setting up income-generating projects as well as addressing health and education issues.[34] Four decades later, the solutions offered by these NGOs have had very little lasting impact.

In 1993, a newspaper reporter observed that 130 000 children lived on the streets of Nairobi,[35] and that the mayor had indicated that both citizens and the government should take 'mutual responsibility' for them. The same reporter noted that the city council, the Undugu Society of Kenya (an NGO that works with street children and homeless adults) and other organisations had decided to accept this challenge. As a result, the Undugu Society initiated the Nairobi Cares for its Children Programme, encouraging supporters to buy coupons from supermarkets which would then donate food to selected rehabilitation centres for street children.

Meanwhile, as recommended by neoliberal policy-makers, municipal services such as water, garbage collection, clinics and housing developments were privatised in the hope that this would create cost savings for the city and increase service-delivery efficiency for citizens. Policy-makers pointed out that competition between private service providers should create a stronger sense of responsibility among employees and thus reduce corruption.[36] What actually happened was that city governance and management continued to deteriorate.

The *East African* reported that Nairobi had sunk into a quagmire. The article painted a picture of councillors engaged in physical fights, internal coups, graft, uncollected garbage and the use of substandard building materials and practices in the city.[37] In another newspaper report, Nairobi is described as filthy: 'Nairobi, the once proud "Green city in the sun" has turned into a capital of filth and neglect – a distant silhouette of what the colonialists bequeathed at independence in 1963'. The report quotes former mayor Charles Rubia as saying, 'We inherited a clean city; we have run it down ourselves through greed, incompetence and a culture of shameless interference by the executive.' Kenya's first mayor from the multiparty era, Steve 'Magic' Mwangi, concurred, highlighting that 'the Ministry of Local Government has played havoc on our local authorities, causing damage that will require billions of shillings to clear up'.[38] In 1997, yet another journalist observed that nothing was working in the city. From traffic lights and revenue collection, traffic management, health services and garbage collection to the maintenance and repair of infrastructure, the city was in disarray.[39]

The crisis was clearly generated by the politically privileged. They had the power to stop the decay but instead oversaw and even supervised further looting. The economy suffered and jobs were steadily lost. The less privileged had little choice but to seek a livelihood using whatever means they could. Unlike in the late 1960s and early 1970s, when the construction of marketplaces had been encouraged and hawkers were being licensed, the city authorities had neither strategies nor processes for handling traders and artisans. As the city's infrastructure deteriorated, so did conditions for traders and artisans. Many were scapegoated for causing disorder and insecurity and they were punished by having their kiosks demolished.

Nairobi in the new millennium

The period from 2001 to 2010 was a time of recovery from the malaise inherited from the city commission and the neoliberal policies introduced by the first multiparty administration. To an extent, discipline was restored, legislation was reviewed and order was enforced in the city. John Gakuo, the town clerk, worked to restore the image of the city. Gakuo was supported by the national minister of local government, Musikari Kombo. Buildings were painted, public parks and gardens were rehabilitated, trees were planted, revenue collection improved, traffic decongestion measures were implemented and floodlights were mounted. Overall, the will to restore and revitalise the city revived.[40]

Emphasis was placed on the use of surveillance and the courts to ensure that municipal bylaws were obeyed. Informal traders and artisans were a major focus of the city clean-up, partly because their built structures tended to obstruct the free flow of traffic and pedestrians. Many families and hawkers were cleared out of the CBD and new regulations were introduced to ensure that individuals could be prosecuted for making the city dirty. In response, market traders in Kangemi undertook to keep their part of the city clean.

From 7 to 13 November 2004, a convention was held to explore ways of making Nairobi safer.[41] The convention emphasised the participatory role of communities and stakeholders in city management. The question of how to deal with hawkers and informal businesses remained a thorny one, particularly when international events were taking place in the city. For example, in 2005, the city authorities again demolished kiosks in preparation for the All Africa Cities Conference, with city officials and the ministry of local government arguing that kiosks provided hideouts for criminals.[42]

The city administration has since attempted to address this by introducing new kiosks. Unfortunately, these are tiny and badly designed so that they get very hot in summer, causing fresh vegetables and fruit to perish rapidly. The city also reconstructed the Muthurwa Market to accommodate hawkers whose presence in the streets was considered a nuisance. Perhaps predictably, many hawkers see the new market as too open and too far away from the CBD where most of their potential customers shop.

Conflicting worldviews

In essence, the problem is that the political and knowledge-privileged elites who govern Nairobi view the city differently from traders and artisans in the informal sector. Schooled mainly in Western institutions or using Western-inspired curricula and learning material, the elites imagine cities of stone buildings and wide, empty pavements. The majority of Kenyans expect cities to contain many homesteads, built of wood, thatch and *mabati* (corrugated-iron sheets). Spatially, these two worldviews generate very different community economies and collective institutions. Issues of overcrowding and the possible problems created by an unregulated sprawl of enterprises are simply not perceived in the same way. For many, it is difficult to understand why one should not 'pull' (add) an extension from a main house to serve as a kiosk or a rented space, or sit in the bright sunlight and open air to sell goods on the street.

In the eyes of the planning and governing elite, the informal economy lacks the corporate structures or limited liability companies to facilitate governability. City planners are generally trained to deal with Western-type enterprise models that are corporate in nature and can be relied on to have names and fixed addresses. By contrast, the presence or otherwise of any particular trader in any single place is generally unpredictable and uncertain. Few traders use company names and they don't all have the stable physical addresses that are crucial for traceability. Traders' ways of conducting business tend to make it difficult to discern regular patterns or practices and the rules and values of informal businesses remain largely unknown. The number and diversity of enterprises further complicates monitoring and management, leading city authorities to argue that instituting effective control measures in relation to informal trade is not economical.

In general, national government business policies have not favoured the traders. Thus, while traders and artisans are still negotiating with the authorities for recognition of their basic right to trade, the multinational and domestic firms belong to the Kenya National Chamber of Commerce and Industry or the Kenya Association of Manufacturers, where they discuss issues of import regulation, taxation, and so on. Corporate bodies are also represented on government committees and their members are awarded accolades and recognition as national heroes.

Meanwhile, multinational firms work hard to control global markets and reap maximum profits which they repatriate to their headquarters in the North. Local firms and parastatals invest much of their time and resources playing catch-up with their transnational competitors. Traders, artisans and peasant farmers struggle to take back some influence over the economy and infuse it with African logic, norms and values.

Put differently, the prevailing economic context in Kenya creates a situation where transnational, domestic and parastatal corporations keep wages low for the majority of workers and deploy their surpluses outside of the country and the continent. This inhibits the growth of a motivated labour force capable of enhancing the productivity of Kenya's economy. The deployment of surpluses abroad means that few investments are made in domestic research and development, and Kenya is failing to generate a critical mass of creative people capable of driving the innovation necessary for enhanced productivity. Domestic firms prefer to buy and import technology rather than invest in local knowledge infrastructure, while traders, artisans and peasant farmers have to weave their way through policies that favour multinational and domestic firms. This policy bias is present because the Kenyan government is, in turn, playing catch-up with the agendas set by the economic powers located in the North (Mkandawire 2014) and, more recently, in the East, as seen in the drafting of *Kenya Vision 2030: A Globally Competitive and Prosperous Kenya* (Republic of Kenya 2007). Kenya's government is simply not interested in taking back or indigenising its economy in ways that might favour the development of local innovators or benefit existing traders and artisans.

Chapter 4 explores how African cities are (mis)understood in the literature on urban development, and begins to explain how informal traders and artisans have shaped urban African spaces.

Chapter 4

Urban theory and the 'African metropolis'

In this chapter, I outline existing theoretical and analytical frameworks that have attempted to explain the phenomenon of traders and artisans in the 'African metropolis'. I review theories about African cities and show that the business practices of traders and artisans can be viewed as both a business model and a strategy for organising autonomous communities in specific territorial complexes. I argue that traders and artisans should be given a voice in city-planning processes because they represent, and have decades of experience in sustaining, an authentically African process of urban formation.

Theorising African cities

African cities attract a significant amount of attention from development practitioners and urban theorists. The poverty and inequality, the dilapidated nature and haphazard location of many buildings, combined with high levels of crime, unemployment, informal trade, poor governance and socio-cultural fragmentation have long been issues of concern. Their generally dystopian condition means that African cities are often seen as 'rogue', 'unformed', 'stragglers' and 'failures', with their citizens as barely surviving the 'urban curse' (Bekker & Fourchard 2013; Pieterse & Simone 2013).

In truth, no urban theory yet developed has been adequate to the task of explaining why cities in Africa are as they are.

Theories developed in the North present African cities as strange and different from cities in Europe, North America and Asia. The poverty, poor infrastructure, weak governance and political dynamics seem difficult to explain. Refreshingly, Robinson (2002, 2013), Robinson and Parnell (2012) and Roy (2009, 2011) question the applicability of contemporary urban theory and the extent to which it explains the evolution of cities in low-income countries outside of the West. They all assert the need for theories that help explain the unique attributes of cities in the South without using Western cities as their main points of reference.

Robinson's (2002) paper entitled 'Global and world cities: A view off the map' challenges the division of cities into global or world cities and non-global or developing cities. She calls for a non-developmentalist approach that acknowledges the ordinariness and cosmopolitan nature of all cities. In later work, Robinson (2013) observes that many types of cities exist and that it is difficult to conceptualise them using any single universal theory. Suggesting that cities be theorised in the context of the 'urban now', she challenges the notion that cities have to be viewed in terms of modernity and innovation or classified as archetypes, stereotypes or prototypes, noting that these lenses privilege some cities over others. Her 'urban now' perspective aims to recraft the relationship between urban outcomes and conceptualisations of the urban by drawing attention to the multiplicity of urban spaces that exist as well as to 'the deeply interconnected nature of cities in the context of global urban processes' (Robinson 2013: 8).

Following a similar track, Roy (2009, 2011) has attempted to explain the evolution of cities in the South. Viewing the development of Southern cities as different from those in the North, she suggests linking the genesis of African cities to urban economies based on the circulation of race, migrants, values, commodities and beliefs (Roy 2009). Roy presents African cities as fluid and characterised by mobile populations. To some extent, however, this view negates the efforts of urban Africans to make cities their dwelling places and undermines the agency they demonstrate while negotiating their livelihoods and creating autonomous communities.

Roy (2011) also attempts to examine whether the economic informality present in cities in the South generally (and Africa in particular) helps to illuminate their evolution. Asking whether 'slum-dog cities' or subaltern urbanism should form the basis of a Southern theory of urbanism, Roy builds on Spivak's (2005) critique of the lack of identity in the term 'subaltern'. She argues that the term 'subaltern' implies that lines of social mobility are located elsewhere, and therefore do not permit the formation of a recognisable basis of action. She also articulates the need for a theory of Southern urbanism that can explain the heterogeneity of megacities without universalising the impact of colonialism or, as Roy puts it, without 'the worlding of the colonial wound' (2011: 231). To this end, Roy proposes that informality be studied through the prism of peripheries, urban informality, zones of exception and grey spaces. She questions whether the entrepreneurship and political agency of the subaltern can really be celebrated in Southern cities, noting her perceptions of a mostly top-down elite-led urbanism rather than processes in which subalterns are free to use their agency to shape institutions in ways that help them fit in and claim cities as their own.

Having experienced street life in Dakar, Senegal and Jakarta, Simone (2013) argues that Southern cities are 'yet to be' and that uncertainty is the 'heart of urbanism'. While it is plausible for Simone (2013) to state that people in African cities live at a junction between cultures, it is important to affirm that many of these same people have some agency to choose where to settle. They can choose, for example, to live in places where they have the agency to create autonomous communities, in which their culture is respected and they can negotiate a livelihood. That is, urban residents are not just bodies in circulation, heading to unknown destinations; they are people with norms, values and logic. They often creatively adorn the spaces they live in, they celebrate their culture, and they name places in ways that define their presence, ownership, relationships or period in history. In all these ways, they leave an imprint on the urban space economy. Turok (2014: 70) observes that, in many African cities,

> Well-endowed political and economic elites and expatriates employed by foreign oil and mining corporations inflate the price of housing, vehicles, consumer goods and food. A surge in the amount of money in circulation ... encourages speculative land acquisition, and luxury property development in addition to a flood of imports ... Inflated property costs and higher consumer prices constrain the growth of domestic industry and raise the cost of living for ordinary citizens. Uncertain property rights and informal transfer systems can also cause distortions such as housing market bubbles.

In my view, this description denies city residents' agency and resilience in responding to their conditions and to the exploitation of resources by the elite. It also fails to acknowledge the ways in which resources flow between the urban and rural areas. For example, an expatriate might employ a domestic worker who in turn invites her brother to the city and helps him start a business in a local market. The brother might purchase stock from a trader in the wholesale market who obtains produce from a farmer. All of the individuals in this network use their earnings to pay for their children's education and several of these children might later find employment in multinational firms. My point is that urban circuits are not limited to inflated prices and land-tenure practices.

Mbembe and Nuttall (2004) also challenge the tendency to view African cities solely through the lenses of urbanisation, modernity and crisis. They highlight the need to understand the various forms of capital that circulate in African cities. They describe Johannesburg as a metropolis that exhibits characteristics of the money economy and individuality. As they point out,

> Johannesburg is peopled not just by workers, the poor, criminals and illegal immigrants but also by civic-minded public intellectuals of all races, highly skilled migrants, jetsetters and new black elite. It

is a home to corporate headquarters, finance houses, legal services, accounting firms, media outlets, entertainment industries and information technology ventures. (Mbembe & Nuttall 2004: 366)

Johannesburg is therefore similar to metropolises described by leading urban theorists such as Max Weber, Georg Simmel and Walter Benjamin. In other words, it is difficult to rule Johannesburg out as a city. This implies that a deeper appreciation of the complexity and diversity of African cities is required. Africa's cities should not be read just in terms of slums and disorder but also through the many diverse processes that are shaping them and how these processes are generating an interacting whole.

Infrastructural and governance challenges

Parnell and Pieterse (2014) bring in the role of infrastructure. They explain that the condition of infrastructure and associated services in African cities is the result of several complex scenarios.

> At the moment most African ... urban residents are structurally trapped in profoundly unhealthy conditions that impact negatively on productivity, economic efficiencies and market expansion. As a consequence of sluggish economic performance, the tax base in African cities remains limited and fragile, making it difficult for governments to raise the revenues necessary to address the litany of urban ills referred to here. Yet the global economy is shifting its axis to the emerging powers. At the same time there is a broader shift towards a fundamentally different much more resource efficient economy and technological opportunities are emerging to fuse citizenship and urban living; within this context, the African urban transition could be truly revolutionary. However, this demands a different scholarly agenda to what has been the norm for some time. The rise of Africa's cities will not be ignored. How the revolution is navigated will depend on how well the forces of change are understood and taken up. In this regard, the role of the continent's intellectuals in framing the debate about cities must be underscored. (Parnell & Pieterse 2014: 15)

The infrastructure and service challenges in cities such as Nairobi are due to lack of ingenuity occasioned by creativity-stifling educational and cultural systems. Rote learning creates planning zombies who copy designs from the West and the East and transpose them onto the local economy. Kenya's educational curricula do little to encourage creativity, problem solving, or the use of imagination. The notion of Africa needing to 'catch up' with the rest of the world is seldom questioned. The assumption is that every country in the world should aspire to the levels of infrastructure prevalent in high-income countries, in which every household has access to at least one car and a washing machine. This assumption creates a sense of failure and deprivation rather than inspiring alternative ways of allocating resources that might be more consistent with community values, as well as more energy efficient and environmentally sustainable.

Governance is another area where urban theory falls short when it comes to explaining African cities. Poor governance and the concomitant powerlessness of urban African citizens is well documented (Bekker & Fourchard 2013). Various kinds of power struggles impact on governance and affect the delivery of services and infrastructure. City authorities often seem to acquire power through gerrymandering and political parties are characterised by their clientelist practices and the intimidation of political opponents. In many cases, metropolitan governance supersedes or sidelines elected metropolitan councils.

In his attempt to develop a theoretical analysis of African cities, Myers (2011: 102) proposes that analysts should focus on resolving the planning dilemmas. He argues that,

> In all cases, at the surface, cities seem to face choices among some kind of Afropolis where informality would be the organising logic; a De Soto-land of formalised informality; or – the likeliest scenario – hybrid understandings that more comfortably weave together the already interpenetrating organizing logics.

Other theorists stress that African cities are strange and badly behaved because of their inability to cope with the emergent socio-political and economic pressures arising from rapid urbanisation. Commenting on what city-making in Africa is about, Ernstson et al. (2014) state that writings on African cities tend to create a frictionless image of African cities as failed, hopeless, dysfunctional and in need of help. In other quarters, urbanisation in Africa has been described as unruly, unpredictable, surprising, and confounding (Pieterse & Simone 2013).

The 'African cities behaving badly' paradigm is confirmed by Mike Davis' *Planet of Slums* (2004) and by UN-Habitat's (2010) *State of the World's Cities* report, both of which characterise African cities as wracked by poverty and violence. While Southern urban theorists have addressed issues related to governance, human migration as well as physical and social infrastructure as factors that differentiate African cities from others, they fail to suggest what drives the different forms that urbanisation takes in Africa. It is not plausible to argue that the differences are attributable to poverty alone.

Scott and Storper (2014) attempt to solve this conundrum by arguing that urbanisation is a product of the dynamics of agglomeration and polarisation that occur at the nexus of location, land use and human interaction. They outline five factors that differentiate cities:

1. *Overall levels of economic development.* Cities in contrasting developmental contexts display widely contrasting profiles in such matters as their economic base, infrastructural endowments and complements of high-, middle- and low-income residents.
2. *Rules that govern resource allocation.* Societies that allocate resources through markets generally do so differently from those that deal with resource allocation using non-market criteria or through a hybrid arrangement, such as a market system combined with robust planning and policy regulations.
3. *Social stratification.* This can be based on class and/or include racial and ethnic variations and has a powerful impact on neighbourhood formation.

4. *Cultural norms and traditions.* These affect a multitude of practices that shape the urban landscape, including the formation, evolution and persistence of neighbourhoods and the ways in which local labour markets operate.

5. *Political authority and power.* Besides having a strong impact on the dynamics of local political contestation, political power typically defines the scope of local government and urban planning, thus influencing the detailed spatial functioning of the urban land nexus.

Scott and Storper's points are particularly relevant to understanding African cities through a prism that highlights the role of traders and artisans in shaping the African metropolis. As shown in later chapters, traders and artisans are one channel through which resources flow into and out of Nairobi. This has led to a particular agglomeration and polarisation of capital and labour in space. However, juxtaposed alongside Western and Oriental business practices and city-planning models, the businesses run by traders and artisans have often been dismissed as inferior and even criminalised. Consequently, they have been denied space and opportunity for incorporation into mainstream urban planning.

Unpacking informality

The continued dominance of traders and artisans in marketplaces in African cities is unmistakable and astounding. Generally, however, such traders have always been studied through the rubric of informality. Informality is a global phenomenon but its dominance in Africa is echoed in a number of studies (see Ernstson et al. 2014; Heintz 2012; Jenkins 2014; Kamete 2013; Kinyanjui 2014; Lindell 2010; Macharia 1997; Myers 2011; Simone 2001; Steck et al. 2013).

The reasons for the dominance of economic informality and inequality in African cities is a major source of speculation. As Parnell and Pieterse (2014: 10) put it,

Poverty, informality and the absence of a strong local state with clear and unchallenged mandate to manage the city are arguably the leitmotifs of African urbanism today. The most telling illustration is the extremely high level of slum living conditions in Africa, compared to other regions in the global south.

Meanwhile, Jenkins (2014) observes that two-thirds of households surveyed in Maputo are linked to the monetary economy through engagement with the informal economy. Jenkins defines the informal economy as comprising enterprises that are not formally contracted and measured or regulated by government, but that residents are daily involved in via vending and small-scale ventures in the city.

Turok (2014) notes that informal enterprises seldom generate incomes that sustain households or contribute enough taxes to national or city coffers to support the large-scale infrastructure needed for public services. He observes that informal enterprises are unable to generate decent jobs, leading most actors in this sector to subsist in precarious conditions of destitution and disaffection. This implies that popular or informal economies are too fluid and fragmented to bring meaningful development to cities. From this perspective, informality in African cities is a stumbling block to growth and development, and it should be done away with.

Certainly, economic informality in African cities does not conform to well-known forms of wage labour or to production for commodity markets or capitalist enterprises (Lipton 1982; Portes et al. 1989). As Hart (1973) points out, the informal sector is remarkably different to the formal sector; it is also seldom recognised by national laws, especially those pertaining to land and property rights (De Soto 1989). Maloney (1999, 2004) notes that labour-market dynamics are another factor that differentiates informal from formal economies. Bromley (1978) and Moser (1978) attribute the sector's origin and survival to its articulation with large capital, while Bangura (1994) suggests that the failure of capitalism's growth-oriented neoliberal policies is responsible for its persistence.

Of course, constructing analytical or theoretical frameworks based on how they differ from the dominant form of capitalist production is problematic. A business model that has not been allowed to work cannot fairly be compared with one that has been supported initially by force and subsequently through aggressive policies backed up by fear and intimidation.

Towards an alternative view of informality

Offering a slightly different view, Gudeman (2001) suggests that the informal sector is a remnant of traditional indigenous methods of organising economies in countries that struggle for ascendancy in the context of modernisation, neoliberalism and the digital revolution. This view is affirmed by my research (see Kinyanjui 2014). It can be argued that actors in the informal economy have resisted capture and incorporation by Western and Oriental business models. The questions that remain relevant are: Why is informality averse to capture? What factors contribute to its struggle for ascendancy? And how do these factors play out in Africa's rural and urban economies? Before attempting to respond to these questions, I briefly sketch some conceptualisations of traditional African views on business.

In 1912, Du Bois attempted to describe an Afrocentric model of doing business in his article 'The upbuilding of black Durham'. He observes that in the 19th century, African Americans in the city of Durham, North Carolina, had created a 'group economy' to support their livelihoods. Du Bois highlights the interdependence and cooperation that existed between the participants as follows:

> It is a new 'group economy' that characterizes the rise of the Negro American – the closed circle of social intercourse, teaching and preaching, buying and selling, employing and hiring, and even manufacturing, which, because it is confined chiefly to Negroes, escapes the notice of the white world. (Du Bois 1912: 334)[43]

More recently, Van den Heuvel (2008) offered some insight into the nature of Afrocentric business model as conceptualised within an *African management movement* that evolved in South Africa in the late 1980s, as the apartheid regime entered its final years.[44] The movement sought to incorporate the traditional values of ubuntu including compassion, cooperation, solidarity and community into corporate management in South Africa. This includes fostering a participatory management style and a humanistic approach to leadership. It also endeavours to acknowledge the humiliation, deprivation and discrimination that Africans experienced under apartheid. Linked to this, Bhengu made some headway in foregrounding African economic philosophy in his book *African Economic Humanism* (2011). Bhengu demonstrates how the values of community, sharing and generosity that are intrinsic to ubuntu are fundamental to African notions of economics.

In my own work, I have proposed that the notion of 'solidarity entrepreneurialism' can help explain African business behaviour (see Kinyanjui 2013, 2014). I use the term solidarity entrepreneurialism to describe the kinds of group agency and individual initiatives in business transactions I have observed among women traders in Nairobi. Here, individual initiative comprises a trader's or artisan's willpower, capacity and commitment to running a business. Group agency covers the ways in which they embrace a community spirit in business transactions, choosing to work with family or friends from the same ethnic group, and to share the risks and transaction costs involved in doing business.

A concept geared towards developing a new African business model is 'Africapitalism'. Developed by Nigerian millionaire and former investment banker Tony Elumelu, Africapitalism is an attempt to exhort wealthy Africans to help transform the continent by investing in strategic sectors with the aim of creating social and economic prosperity. According to Elumelu,

> The term 'Africapitalism' describes the process of transforming private investment into social wealth. As homegrown businesses meet social and economic needs by creating goods and services with an innate understanding of the local environment, they can bring private capital to vital infrastructure like road transport and power generation. And they can create jobs for Africans, which

will in turn create an African middle class – a new generation of African consumers.[45]

These approaches (Du Bois' group economy, the African management movement, solidarity entrepreneurialism and Africapitalism) represent attempts to find an Afrocentric business philosophy. Their existence suggests that although modernity is ever encroaching, some traditional forms of African logic, norms and values remain present in contemporary business practice.

Rethinking the role of traders and artisans

In my experience, traditional African markets are relational and creative spaces that show a surprising degree of social harmony. Founded on the bedrock of African logic, norms and values, they persist despite having been stifled by modernist city planning and neoliberal imaginaries. They demonstrate a creative alternative to the dominant capitalist model, while fostering spatial and relational forms that are as yet little understood in African urbanism.

As shown earlier in this book, the current spaces of economic informality in Nairobi are directly related to indigenous markets that have existed there since the city was founded in the 1890s (see also Kinyanjui 2014). Quickly marginalised by the colonial authorities as hawkers, and since relegated the 'informal economy', few have attempted to understand Nairobi's traders and artisans on their own terms. Without this, however, economic informality in that city cannot be fully understood. Similarly, Ikioda (2013) demonstrates the important role that market traders play in meeting the needs of Nigeria's urban populations and proposes that the role of Africa's urban markets in development be investigated.

In fact, Africa's urban markets had already attracted significant scholarship in the 1960s and 1970s. Hodder (1969) describes African markets as meeting points for buyers and sellers. Riddell (1974), in a study of markets in Sierra Leone, observes that these were important for the circulation of food and crafts. Riddell observed that the markets were highly organised, with systematic spatial and temporal patterns, and played an important economic role in the purchase and exchange of commodities. He noted that the markets also played a key social role by providing spaces for people to meet and communicate. On their impact, Riddell noted that markets in Sierra Leone could be seen as an index of modernisation and represented a truly African response to processes of change in that country. Most studies done in the 1960s and 1970s tended to view markets in a similarly positive light. This perception has since been lost (Robertson 1997).

It was at the start of the neoliberal era in the late 1980s that traders and artisans became seen as vulnerable entrepreneurs struggling to adapt to the realities of neoliberalism and needing to be educated about business development. In much development discourse and practice, traders and artisans were seen as needing to be rescued from themselves. International development agencies initiated development programmes and supported NGOs to render various services aimed at doing just that (see Burbank 1994; Mullei and Bokea 1999; Namusonge 1999). Traders and artisans were offered courses in entrepreneurship, business development, marketing and bookkeeping by a range of NGOs. Meanwhile, financial institutions offered credit using Muhammad Yunus's Grameen Bank micro-finance model, which involves giving loans to groups rather than individuals (Namusonge 1999). However, while one might have expected these NGOs and micro-financiers to situate their offices in marketplaces where concentrations of traders and artisans are high, this has never been the case. As a result, such business-development and credit services have yet to reach a critical mass of traders and artisans in African markets.

From about 2010, interest in African markets surged again. In a study of Dantokpa Market in Cotonou, Benin, Prag (2010) demonstrates that the market occupies an important place in the urban economy, generating a substantial amount of income for the city via taxes, tolls and other funds. Prag notes that the market also plays a political role, showing that by allying itself with a network of poorer traders and women, the government has been able to fend off the political opposition. The main traders' network relies on the authority of traditional chiefs who support the state. This network also strongly opposes the modernisation and formalisation of the market, and employ trusted village kin as security guards rather than modern security companies. A smaller but wealthier and more successful group of traders, who belong mainly to the Adja community, support both modernisation and the political opposition. These tensions ensure that Dantokpa Market is central to political mobilisation in Cotonou. Prag (2010: 22) concludes, therefore, that the market is a 'nest of political patrons', and that the government strives to control the market to ensure that it does not lose ground to the opposition.

Prag also describes how the market had been an incubator for evolution of the now wealthier Adja traders, noting that they had once been apprenticed to the Yoraba traders. The Adja learned to trade, and through intensive networking and solidarity, they were able to dominate the trade in vehicle spare parts. Gradually, they became strong enough to break away from larger trader networks and join the political opposition.

The notion of indigenous economic practices and value systems as offering economic alternatives is yet to be appreciated in societies that have experienced the effects of Polanyi's great transformation (see Chapter 1). Since the colonial invasions, indigenous economic practices and transactions in Africa have been portrayed as obstacles to this transformation. 'Development', via colonialism, neoliberalism or the adoption of South East Asian policies and strategies, has been prescribed as a likely remedy at different times. Associated 'medication' has included acculturation, the opening up of free trade and promises of massive investments in infrastructure which invariably fail to materialise.

Instead, the application of all of these 'remedies' has massively interfered with and interrupted existing African economic ethics and relationships, creating a conflict between those who embrace indigenous African values in relation to doing business and those who do not. Those who embrace indigenous values are described as being part of the informal or traditional economy while those who embrace the dominant global system are considered part of the formal economy, and as being on the road to development.

The cultural domination occasioned by colonialism distorted African people's identities and moral values – key ingredients for economic development. Iroegbu (n.d.) observes that Africans have always used their culture to uplift themselves. Thus, despite their lack of access to modern education and their alleged backwardness in the context of urban modernity, they have not only survived but also shown enormous resilience in the face of countless obstacles. Iroegbu argues that the wisdom of African culture manifests in the traditions that characterise family occasions and religious practices as well as in an urban cosmology of survival and resilience.

While the cultural conflict generated by colonialism and neoliberal economics has been depicted in works of fiction such as Okot p'Bitek's *Song of Lawino* (1966), and in autobiographies such as R Mugo Gatheru's *A Child of Two Worlds* (1966) and Ali Mazrui's *The Africans: A Triple Heritage* (1986), documentation on its effects on African economic values and practices is scarce. In general, academic discourse, as well as the dominant culture and media, has imposed a kind of dystopian vision on anything African, be it economic, social or political. This vision overshadows the resilience and social innovations that ordinary people develop every day as they live their lives and it denies Africans any entitlement to their own past, present or future.

Africans' economic logic and institutions have long been ignored or treated with disdain. Ochieng Odhiambo provides the following example of how early 19th-century writings disparaged Africans' way of doing business and managing everyday life:

The negro has but a few gifts for endeavours and tasks that aim at a distant goal and requires tenacity, independence and foresight. He has never succeeded in larger undertakings, which needs a plan for a far future and a wider view of casting on a large scale. He works from day to day without a clear picture and vision of the consequences; he lives his days as they come, day by day. (quoted in Ochieng Odhiambo 1995: 9)

With minds and eyes clouded by the colonialist view of Africa, development experts and international financial institutions have endeavoured to promote entrepreneurship among Africans as if Africa has never had any business logic, ethos or practices of its own. Prior to colonial domination and exploitation, Africans traded among themselves and with their neighbours, as the trans-Saharan trade routes and the long-distance trade of the Nyamwezi make clear. Trade with the Arabs and Chinese was well established, and after the 15th century, some trade occurred with Europeans.

Knowing this, it seems incredible that contemporary research on small enterprises by students at Kenya's business schools still problematises the challenges facing small businesses rather than exploring how small business owners manoeuvre around the problems they face. At best, entrepreneurs who run small businesses are presented as helpless, hopeless or criminal, and the business environment is presented as a space in which small enterprises labour to get by rather than one of resilience, thriving and self-fulfilment. For example, the online catalogue at the University of Nairobi's library contains 673 entries that refer to articles and books on the challenges of small businesses. Here the dystopia of the small-business environment is captured in titles such as 'The messy reality of agglomeration economies in urban informality: Evidence from Nairobi's handicraft industry' (Harris 2014). As McCormick (1999) points out, small businesses are often described as being in a state of 'waiting', 'yet to be' or 'on the way to becoming'.

Such research successfully catalogues and glorifies the problems experienced by small enterprises rather than creating an understanding of the processes involved in creating these businesses and their *raison d'être* (Kinyanjui 2007). In this way, the agency that traders and artisans have, and the willpower that they use every day, is negated. Hordes of development agencies, practitioners and consultants use these academic works to justify creating a multitude of training programmes aimed at 'rescuing' traders and artisans from the hazards of economic informality.

Despite all this, economic informality continues to flourish and thrive in Africa's cities and the pre-existing logics, norms and values that have been developed and shared by traders and artisans for aeons remain undocumented and unexplored. Traders and artisans have survived and constantly reinvented themselves in the cities. Markets remain significant in defining urban imaginaries because they are a source of wealth, they are centres of learning and are run according to rules and regulations. Traders and artisans help to influence the flow of goods and services, shape human interaction in the city, and determine patterns of accumulation in the built environment. Analysis of these aspects of urbanism needs to go beyond existing urban theory and urban planning.

Work, production and the shaping of urban space

Scott and Storper (1986) usefully analyse the dynamic role of production and work, the key tenets of industrial capitalism, in generating territories in Europe and North America. They clearly demonstrate the nexus that exists between production and work in generating specific kinds of territories and shaping space. As they put it, 'territory (i.e. humanly differentiated geographical space) is a creature of those forces that underlie the material reproduction of social life and that find their immediate expression in various forms of production and work' (Scott & Storper 1986: 301). In other words, cities are agglomerations of labour and capital where technological changes are generated, divisions of labour are evolved and affective political expressions of communal life find a place.

Scott (2011) observes how concentrations of labour and capital have contributed to the evolution of cities, and identifies three scenarios in which cities have evolved under capitalism. He shows how, in the 19th century, manufacturing towns evolved as a result of the factory and workshop system in Britain. In the mid-20th century, large metropolitan areas in North America grew up under the Fordist manufacturing era. Scott argues that, currently, global city regions are evolving under what he calls 'cognitive cultural capitalism'. Such cities are populated by employees of high-technology industries who tend to be well educated and creative and a servile class of workers who have lower levels of education, many of whom are labour migrants.

In line with this theory that different concentrations of labour and capital have a bearing on emergent urbanism, it is useful to apply the insights of Scott and Storper (1986) and Scott (2011) to the ways in which traders and artisans engage in production and distribution and contribute to concentration of capital and labour. In later chapters, I describe how the concentration of capital and labour inherent in the development of Nairobi's markets has contributed to the evolution of that African metropolis. I also show how the markets regulate traders' and artisans' investment behaviours, shape the physical infrastructure and drive divisions of labour as well as new learning and innovation in their communities.

Focusing more on how markets contribute to urban development and have the potential to shape the culture and identity of different areas within urban spaces, Grabski (2012) illustrates that the growth of the Colobane arrondissement in Dakar is directly attributable to the presence of Colobane Market. As the market expanded, so did the community surrounding it. Grabski shows that the market is an important space for economic mobility and for facilitating both the convergence and divergence of people and culture.

Ehinmowo and Ibitoye (2010) observe that in Akoko, Nigeria, marketplace trade is dominated by women and that a gender division exists between the products that men and women sell. Women largely sell cereal crops, potatoes and vegetables, while men sell meat. Masaru and Badenoch (2013) observe that markets are important in maintaining everyday life in villages, acting as centres of economic vibrancy and cultural diversity as well as developing specialised niche products linked to certain villages.

Ikioda (2013) observes that marketplaces are becoming increasingly important in different parts of the world. In the United States, markets are used to promote racial diversity and public interaction, while in Europe, markets have long been meeting points for communities, and for the exchange of both goods and ideas. Nowadays, European markets in both urban areas and rural villages serve as focal points for the sale of healthy local produce, as centres for innovation in the design and manufacture of high-end handmade goods, and as spaces for social gatherings. In Lagos, markets meet a range of needs for the urban population: they are a source of employment and income for many people, especially women, who work as traders, porters, couriers and security guards. Markets also sustain vital links between rural and urban areas.

Despite these studies, Ikioda (2013) points out that too many development practitioners have failed to recognise the important role markets play in Africa, continuing to present them as unruly and primitive and therefore in need of formalisation and modernisation. A similar failure to understand the economic role played by markets is evident in Kenya's business schools. These institutions strive to promote Western and Chinese business ethics and models, while downplaying the vital role of African indigenous markets in harnessing labour and capital in Kenyan cities. In general, the role of markets in mobilising African communities into urbanisation is still underestimated by modernist discourse, which describes the markets as archaic and backward, filled with traders who barely subsist and are unable to lift themselves out of poverty (Ikioda 2013).

As Grabski (2012) demonstrates, the Colobane Market affects the imaginary of the artists in Dakar, Senegal as well as raising the living standards of the community in which it is based. Guyer (2015), too, illustrates that the markets serve vital functions including generating employment, circulating money, stimulating innovation and ensuring skills transfer. All this, and yet many still see African markets as peripheral to urban and national economies.

In reality, markets are a hallmark of Africa. Men and women, young and old share space, sitting or standing side by side, selling anything from the latest Chinese garments to sweet potatoes, household utensils and farm implements. As Grabski (2012) puts it: 'you can find anything in the world in Colobane Market'. Markets provide opportunities for income generation, for people to move between the urban and rural worlds, and to widen their networks. Their periodicity marks both the days of the week and the seasons. Market days are seen as special days on which people converge to trade, chat, receive news and buy things to prepare for long journeys. This is where surplus from the farms is sold on and artisans bring their crafts. When I was growing up, market days did not just happen; they were pre-arranged and space was set apart for them. Markets were also open and free to all despite having clear rules and regulations. In addition to being places of production and exchange, markets play a religious and political role.

Engrossed in the pursuit of modernity, academics, policy planners, economic analysts and development experts have disregarded the uniquely African attributes evident in the organising of African economies. The notion of informality has been imposed on many of Africa's economic practices, and these have been judged as sources of the stasis preventing African economies from industrialising and undergoing structural transformation (see Hart 1973; Lewis 1954). For example, La Porta and Shleifer (2014) describe the traditional sector in African economies as permanently informal and lacking in dynamism because it is cash based, with the hiring of labour as well as the buying and selling of goods mostly happening with cash. In this way, scholars and development practitioners have failed to recognise the historical and cultural factors that informed the evolution of these businesses. Rather than seeing the economic behaviours of traders and artisans as a viable business model, academic and development discourse has ignored their logic, norms and values.

Despite the countless obstacles placed in their paths over many decades, Nairobi's traders and artisans have continued to enshrine and embody African business logic, ethics, norms and values. In other countries, too, they compete effectively with Western businesses in African cities (see Wegerif 2014). They do not deserve to be wished away or ignored in (mis)understandings of urban transformation in Africa. As Gibson-Graham (2006: 59) suggests, it is time to 'step outside of the condensing and displacing powers of capitalocentrism and give the full diversity of economic relations and practices the space to exist in all their specificity and independence'.

Part Two
The Making of an African City

Chapter 5

The indigenisation of Nairobi

In the previous chapter, I noted that African economic logic, norms and values remain deeply rooted in Nairobi. The resilience of the city's traders and artisans has created a subtle and subliminal indigenisation process that has been integral to the evolution of the city. This process of indigenisation has seldom been grounded in official policies, and has largely been driven by ordinary citizens.

In this chapter, I first describe some of indigenisation policies implemented in postcolonial Africa and specifically in Nairobi. I then show how these policies conflicted with other planning and economic imperatives and were shelved by the authorities. Since the 1990s, a range of individual and community initiatives have gradually brought indigenisation back into the spotlight in Nairobi, albeit not officially and with little backing from the city authorities.

Postcolonial urban planning in Africa

As they achieved independence in the mid-1960s and began trying to claw their way back to economic health, most African governments started searching for a planning paradigm that would affirm their Africanness in political and economic terms, both locally and globally. They seem to have explored three options for achieving this: using state resources, attracting foreign investment and foreign aid, and reverting to an indigenous or traditional African model of doing business.

Different countries were effectively coerced into adopting different combinations of the first two options even though they might have preferred the third. As president of Ghana, Kwame Nkrumah called for a unified Africa that would share infrastructure to address the legacies of underdevelopment. Julius Nyerere, while president of Tanzania, implemented ujamaa, a social policy intended to uphold African values of solidarity and communality. He encouraged the formation of village cooperatives based on equal opportunity and self-sufficiency. Kenneth Kaunda, as president of Zambia, proposed a form of humanism that places the good of humanity at the centre of all state activities.

However, it was not easy for Africans to find a balance between adopting Western values and retaining African ones. In the late 1950s and well into the 1960s, development thinking recommended that the rest of the world catch up with the industrialised nations through modernisation rather than indigenisation. Scholars such as Lewis (1954) recommended that the dual nature of traditional and non-traditional economies be dealt with and McClelland (1961) argued that tradition held back development.

Kenya, like many other African countries, faced major problems as it tried to recover from massive economic, social and cultural damage done by decades of colonial exploitation. Development policies that emphasised the need to catch up with Europe and North America in terms of urbanisation, education, economics and politics were initiated through five-year plans. As African governments pursued this catch-up agenda, they progressively abandoned African values.

By the early 1970s, scholars such as Rodney (1972) began to point out how trade relations with Europe were reinforcing Africa's economic dependency and exploitation. African countries seemed hell-bent on using the industrialisation to chart their development path but were massively constrained by their lack of financial and technical resources. While Rodney (1972) suggested that Africa sever ties with Europe, Mazrui (1986) demonstrated the complexity of what it means to be African. Mazrui argues that it is not practical to claim Africanness on the basis of geography alone, observing that Africans are heirs to a triple legacy – African, Islamic and Western. He suggests that the legacies of these three civilisations are so entrenched in Africans' everyday lives, perceptions and negotiations that they can no longer be disentangled.

Kenya has had four presidents since 1964, when the country achieved independence: Jomo Kenyatta (1964–1978), Daniel arap Moi (1978–2002), Mwai Kibaki (2002–2013) and Uhuru Kenyatta (2013–). Kenyatta initiated a brand of African capitalism that combined self-reliance, group investments and private ownership of property. He initiated the spirit of *harambee* (pulling together) as the basis of the country's great transformation. Moi's regime promised to follow in Kenyatta's footsteps but actually did little to disrupt the status quo. Kibaki entrenched classical neoliberalism in Kenya, prioritising individualism and economics. During his reign, the notion of *harambee* was replaced with state-sponsored projects run via his Constituency Development Fund. Unfortunately, the economic policies pursued during the three different administrations benefited only certain sections of the community, fostering a culture of political patronage and corruption that has become key to the dynamics of the national economy (Hydén 1994; Leys 1975).

As Hydén (1994: 85) observes,

[Kenyatta's] strategy was to create a number of parastatals, notably the Industrial and Commercial Development Corporation (ICDC) and the Kenya National Trading Corporation (KNTC) to provide credit and other forms of support to budding entrepreneurs. Much of the demand for these services came spontaneously from the entrepreneurially minded Kikuyu, but the skewed distribution of these benefits was further reinforced by the fact that these bodies were controlled by Kikuyu appointees. With the benefit of hindsight, it is easy to see that this approach led not only to the rapid Africanisation of certain sectors of the economy, notably the retail sector, but also strengthening of Kenyatta's political base.

This observation may hold true for some of the political and educated elite from the Agikuyu[46] community who were close to the regime. Today, the elite are more diverse in terms of ethnicity and manifest spatially in different parts of the city. For example, some parts of Nairobi's built environment might be considered to have 'caught up' with what the global elite aspire to. Estates[47] such as Karen, Westlands, Lavington, Spring Valley, Nyali and Gigiri are very similar to those found in parts of high-income Western or Asian countries. However, for the majority of the city's inhabitants, including traders in markets such as Uhuru, Wakulima, Gikomba and Ngara, this catching-up process has hardly begun. In 2014, the Kenya National Bureau of Statistics estimated that over two million people work in Nairobi's markets (KNBS 2014).

The idea of incorporating indigenous values and practices into urban planning has received some attention in the contemporary era of globalisation. In 2007, the UN began promoting the rights of indigenous communities via its Declaration on the Rights of Marginal and Aboriginal Communities. Subsequently, Australia introduced additional legal rights for indigenous people. In Latin America, the University of the Autonomous Regions of the Nicaraguan Caribbean Coast is connecting students and grassroots community organisations into wider discussions of modernity, colonisation and decoloniality (Sidaway et al. 2014).

Along similar lines, Iyam (2013) has investigated the persistence of certain indigenous traditions even as communities embrace change. Using the example of the fattening rooms linked to marriage traditions in south-eastern Nigeria, Iyam notes that far from being abandoned, such traditions are being integrated with contemporary practices. Iyam suggests that both continuity and change are evident in such cultural practices, and that they help to create a degree of harmony between Western and African norms.

A similar form of integration is reflected in Kenyan marriages, where both African and Western rituals often take place. Usually, a Christian ceremony occurs after the traditional African rites are celebrated. Among the Agikuyu, for example, these include *ruracio* (the paying of bride-price when the groom's family is invited to the bride's family home) and *itara* (the bride's family's reciprocal visit to the groom's home). The reality that these indigenous institutions remain so prevalent among Kenyans suggests the need for wider conversation about how African cultural practices might be better integrated into business and urban development.

Planning in Nairobi from the mid-1960s

Making Nairobi a truly African city was a key objective for the Kenyan government in the first two decades after independence. In 1964, then-minister for local government Ayondo, addressed one of the city council's monthly meetings and advised the council to make Nairobi a truly African city by including all inhabitants of the metropole in their plans. He argued that, up to this point, Nairobi had been a city of the rich that favoured those fortunate enough to have formal employment. He encouraged everyone to look beyond racial, religious and tribal prejudices and urged the council to make everyone feel part of the city.[48]

Imbued with the spirit of liberation, Kenya's newly independent government tried to base its development planning on African logic and values. This was expressed in Sessional Paper 10 of 1965 entitled *African Socialism and its Implications for Planning* (Republic of Kenya 1965). In the paper, the state advocated a political and economic system that was 'positively African'; that is, not overly influenced by foreign blueprints but still capable of accommodating useful models from elsewhere. Key principles were: to draw from the best African traditions; to make the system adaptable to new circumstances and rapid change; and to avoid depending on any country or group of countries for success (Republic of Kenya 1965: 3). African socialism was thus seen as being rooted in African traditions, independent of foreign influence, and based on the universal human values of equity, social justice, human dignity, freedom of conscience as well as freedom from want, disease and exploitation. Political democracy and mutual social responsibility were put forward as key tenets of the system.

According to the sessional paper, African political tradition recognises that individuals are born free and equal and discourages community domination by powerful interest groups. In a traditional context, an individual's voice or counsel is respected regardless of their economic status. 'Even where traditional leaders appeared to have greater wealth and hold disproportionate political influence over their tribal or clan community, there were traditional checks and balances including sanctions against any abuse of such power' (Republic of Kenya 1965: 3). African leaders were seen as trustees of communities in that their modes of administration and management were controlled by religion and customary laws while age and maturity were determining factors for participation in political life (Republic of Kenya 1965).

The critical role of African traditional religion in regulating political behaviour was the main difference between African socialism, communalism and capitalism. African socialism differed from communalism because every mature citizen was seen as having equal political rights. The irrelevance of citizens' personal economic power differentiated the system from capitalism. In addition, social responsibility in African socialism involved the incorporation of the African family spirit in the project of nationhood. Members of society were expected to do their best for each other on the understanding that if society prospered, everyone would benefit. To facilitate this, the state undertook to work towards providing equal opportunities and equal access to social services, such as education, health and social security, as well as to eliminate exploitation and discrimination (Republic of Kenya 1965: 4).

Since every member of African traditional society has a duty to work, the state would try to ensure that every member of the society was gainfully employed. Those who wrote the paper argued that this duty would be acknowledged and willingly accepted by Kenyans as long as mechanisms for sharing the accrued societal benefits were established. Society's reciprocal response to individual contributions was assumed to be definite, automatic and universally accepted (Republic of Kenya 1965: 4).

The sessional paper was heavily criticised by some as unAfrican, socialist and a poor blueprint for development (see Ghai 1965; Obama 1965). Nevertheless, some aspects of the programme were implemented. Nairobi's first mayor, Charles Rubia, was an ardent adherent of African socialism. He was committed to the independence-struggle ideals of self-governance and racial equality. Endeavouring to implement city policy in this spirit, he attempted to Africanise the city administration by employing more Africans. He also made schooling more accessible to Africans, provided decent housing for Africans in the city by opening up new areas such as Kariokor and Madaraka, and made space for African markets. Rubia was often at loggerheads with other councillors over the issue of Africanisation, especially in relation to the treatment of hawkers and beggars. He wanted everyone in the city to be treated with dignity and given access to the means of making a living. First, he made provision for hawkers to sell their goods from designated spaces in the city all day rather than having to keep moving to avoid harassment from police and other city officials. Later, the council decided to construct buildings in these spaces.

Not everyone followed Rubia's example. Instead, some chose to thwart the spirit of African socialism expressed in the sessional paper, taking advantage of their positions in the city or national administrations to enrich themselves. Some allocated themselves large parcels of land in the distribution and settlement projects. Gitu Wa Kahengeri, secretary-general of the Mau Mau War Veterans Association, attributes this to the fact that relatively few of the people who occupied administrative positions after the colonial period had been involved in the independence struggle. Part of the reason for this is that the Africanisation of the civil service, as well as the public and private sectors, began when many of the freedom fighters were still in detention. Recruitment processes also tended to favour those who had been educated in missionary schools (*athomi*). Few of these people had any real respect for traditional African values or even for the values and ideals of self-rule, which might have encouraged them to seek economic justice. They also lacked any loyalty to the aims of the freedom struggle (Interview 2015).

Conflicts between indigenisation and planning

The government's failure to incorporate African values into Kenya's legal system has since fostered conflict. Ideally, each community's own moral fabric should have been integrated into a national moral code of ethics capable of guiding the nation. As Richard Gitau, a farmer and former member of the Mau Mau liberation movement, observes, stark differences exist between how Western jurisprudence and African customary laws are applied in Kenya. For example, Gitau sees the Cooperative Societies Act (No. 2 of 2004) as actually protecting those who swindle and steal from farmers' cooperatives. In African tradition, social rules and regulations dealt with such lawbreakers and made sure that victims were compensated (Interview 2015).

The implications of the deep cultural conflict between the *athomi* (missionary-educated elite) versus the *acenji* (illiterate) for the evolution of indigenisation must not be underestimated. The *athomi* were socialised to disregard African indigenous practices. They were encouraged to reject their parents' values and taught their children to turn their backs on African culture. The distinction between the *acenji* and *athomi* was sharp and their worldviews were virtually impossible to integrate. The division between them played out in the interactions between the city administrators, who were professionally trained, and the city councillors, most of whom were illiterate and had been elected to their positions by local citizens.

In an unpublished report compiled in 1973, Gilbert Njau, a planning officer in Nairobi's city council, made the following observation about urban planning:

> Planning on a comprehensive basis is relatively new in this country. The public therefore must be prepared ... to appreciate the problems and the remedies that are to be employed in order to guide development. Where planning is an alien concept, there is a danger of it being rejected. Even in countries where planning has

been in operation for a long time, there are tendencies of regarding it as a negative exercise and therefore dreaded. (Njau 1973)

In addition, it seems that few if any of the city administrators were fully confident that they could plan for the city. Evidence suggests that they relied instead on experts from outside the country. Senior economists from the UN technical assistance programme were consulted and an urban study group was established. This consisted of UNDP personnel, consultants and was chaired by the provincial commissioner for Nairobi (Njau 1973).

Difficulties that plagued Nairobi's city planners in the 1970s included the lack of planning policies, inadequate financial resources, strong conflicts of interest in the community as a whole as well as opposing priorities within government. The complexity of the planning dilemmas facing the city and the frustrations that planners experienced in trying to implement the relevant legislation are evident in the following extract from Njau's (1973) report:

The city council has functions given to it to perform but we have suffered from general lack of guidelines on policy, for example, on housing. In Zambia, there is a definite policy. We tend to lay our own standards which sometimes conflict with what other people feel is desirable. We operate within financial resources available, not without much opposition in other respects. Markets for example were said to be too elaborate. Some called them white elephants. There is free land in our planning and we have been at loggerheads with some ministries. With regard to development control, this is not usually welcome. Any developer would like to do what he likes. We insist on standards laid down for example on density of population, road thickness, drainage, etc. In this respect, we are unpopular. Considerable pressure is brought to bear but we hide under the law. Many architects are now getting used to principles.

In 1975, conflicts in urban planning and implementation impacted on the authorities' handling of a cholera outbreak. One of the measures taken by the health authorities was to close kiosks used by traders and artisans, thus preventing trade to a large extent.[49] Elected members of parliament who represented ordinary people were up in arms about this. Writing to the city council, Kenya's then-permanent secretary for health, a Mr Boit, decried the fact that the health sector was starved of funding. He also observed that the closure of existing kiosks for traders had created significant political repercussions and asked that 'hygienic' kiosks be built.

Mwangi Mathai, member of parliament for Langata at the time, expressed his frustration with the city planners' inability to acknowledge the role played by traders in reducing the number of people who would otherwise be forced to rely on food welfare.

> My only regret is the fact that recently this sound policy seems to be undergoing some adverse changes that are not in the interest of our people. I certainly take pride in the fact that in Nairobi, cases of those who would seek help from the administration in form of food etc. have reduced due to the fact that our people are able to earn a living this way. There are virtually no beggars to talk about. I was rather perturbed by the latest attitude of the council when recently hawkers were harassed under the pretext of the presence of the cholera epidemic. I was delighted when His Excellency the President intervened and saved what was going to be an explosive situation. I would strongly suggest that your council reconsider as an urgent matter of policy the future security of these hawkers. To allow such a large group of Kenyans to exist under fear and insecurity is tantamount to betrayal of human rights especially when there are reasonable alternatives.
>
> Finally, I would like to refer to the unnecessary requirement by your council that only licensed hawkers themselves should operate their kiosks and be barred from using relatives or employee assistants. This is unfair since these hawkers leave their kiosks closed while in town for normal supplies. This results in loss of revenue to them that is certainly unnecessary. I would suggest that your council re-examines this requirement with a view to easing the situation for these wananchi. In fact, some hawkers could employ a number of people to ease unemployment.[50]

Cultural conflict also had an impact on indigenisation. The work of Mazrui and Gatheru is instructive here. In *The Africans: A Triple Heritage* (1986), Mazrui describes the impact of Islamic, Western and African values on the continent's environment, built infrastructure, religions and economies.[51] In *A Child of Two Worlds*, Gatheru (1966: 2) describes the Agikuyu encounter with British colonialism and the dilemma he faces in juggling his African cultural identity with Western values and norms:

> My people, the Kikuyu are being hammered, beaten, and drawn, too, by the great forces that I have now learned, after my college, to call urbanisation, industrialisation and acculturation. I have learned, too, that I am what the sociologists call a 'marginal man' – a child of two worlds.

Of Nairobi, he writes that there appeared to be two groups in the city, one that regarded the city as a place for making money. The other group seemed to see Nairobi as belonging to Asians and Europeans, and as a place that no African could regard themselves as part of. Their real home was in the rural areas. Africans therefore seemed to see the city as a place for migrants and as 'a means to an end' (Gatheru 1966: 95). These perspectives had significant ramifications for the way the majority of Africans behaved in the city.

> The result was that after working for a considerable number of years in Nairobi, these people would eventually return to the rural area with some money returning to the city only to replenish their income. Some would continue working for a long time but their feeling and security were always in the countryside where they might have owned a small piece of land. Some men had left their wives working on their small holdings in the reserves while they were working in Nairobi. (Gatheru 1966: 95)

In a similar vein, fiction writers, such as Chinua Achebe in *Things fall Apart* (1958), Ngũgĩ Wa Thiong'o in *The River Between* (1965) and Okot p'Bitek in *Song of Lawino* (1966), have documented the clash between African and Western culture, ethics and socio-political institutions. The obliteration of African values portrayed by these writers is symbolised by the deaths of protagonists who represent African tradition (Muthoni in *The River Between* and Okwonkwo in *Things Fall Apart*).

The implications of these cultural conflicts on the spatial organisation of communities in emergent cities, especially with regard to the built environment and different forms of livelihood, remain unexplored. Under colonial rule, the failure of Africans living in Nairobi to lay claim to urban citizenship was attributable to their lack of economic mobility, job insecurity, poor housing conditions, pass laws and the fact that women were prohibited from living in the city.

By the 1980s, this had changed but was still highly contested. A protracted legal battle that took place over the burial of SM Otieno, a prominent Nairobi lawyer, is illustrative of this. Otieno's widow wanted her husband to be buried in Nairobi, in the suburb of Upper Matasia where they had lived.[52] Her husband's side of the family, who were from the Umira Kager clan, wanted him buried at his rural home. A key argument in the legal battle was that individuals have houses *not homes* in cities, and Otieno's clan maintained that his true home was in the rural area.

It remains true that many Africans who die in Nairobi have their bodies transported back to their rural homes of origin as they believe this is where they belong. As I explain in a later chapter, the spatial manifestations of this dual citizenship and identity have an important bearing on the nature of investments that Africans make when they have surplus resources and on where they make these investments. The same issues also have a bearing on emerging businesses and the impact these have on the metropolis.

Between 1963 and 1970, government-initiated efforts to indigenise the city involved building houses with shared courtyards where neighbours could gather if they wanted to, but this project was gradually abandoned. After the first decade of independence, indigenisation seems to have been neglected in both policy and practice. This partly explains why most of the infrastructural and housing development that has occurred in Nairobi since 1970 serves so few of the city's inhabitants. Despite this, however, African logic, norms and values continue to shape the city, and especially the less affluent communities.

Indigenisation by popular demand

In the late 1980s and early 1990s, a revival of interest in African culture began in Nairobi. Among other things, this involved the promotion of African culture, values and architectural forms in parts of the city that were still largely European and Asian in character. This took various forms. For example, in several hotels and restaurants, some enterprising individuals from the village of Rwathia obtained permission to set up Makuti restaurants. These were grass-thatched wooden buildings, some of which were round like African huts, in which African cuisine was served with a range of locally brewed beers. Roasted meats, bone soup and dishes such as *ugali* (corn meal) and *mukimo* (a mash of potatoes, corn and other vegetables) became popular, and several similar restaurants were opened. Since then, other upmarket restaurants, such as Carnivore in Langata, have taken this concept further, hosting 'African nights' and inviting different ethnic groups to showcase their culture. At the time of writing, Osewe's restaurant on Kimathi Street specialises in *ugali* (cooked maize meal) and fish; Watene's on Monrovia Street specialises in *mukimo*, *githeri* (maize and beans), *njahi* (black kidney beans) and *matoke* (cooked bananas). In addition, *ngwaci* (sweet potatoes), *nduma* (arrowroot) and *ugali* now feature on the menus of almost all the cafés and restaurants in the city.

Nelson Wakajuma has a somewhat similar story. In the 1990s, he spent some time in the US, where he saw how people in American cities flocked to flea markets. On his return to Kenya, Wakajuma organised a series of flea markets in Nairobi's city centre (Kinyanjui 2014). These were so successful and so similar to existing African markets that the concept was quickly adopted by other hawkers and traders who, by then, had largely been relegated to trading in the city's outlying suburbs. Traders rented buildings and subdivided them into stalls to such an extent that the entire CBD is sometimes described as one large African market (Kinyanjui 2014).

Another example of neo-traditionalist activities permeating contemporary life is evident in Roman Catholic masses. African melodies and instruments, such as drums and *kayamba* (tambourines), enrich the services; priests wear vestments made from African cloth and some of the newer churches have been designed to resemble the round buildings found in traditional African homesteads. Even some of the multinational corporations have recognised the importance of including African traditions in their marketing programme. A Coca-Cola advertisement, under the slogan 'A billion reasons to believe in Africa', invokes the ethos and principles of solidarity, sharing and reciprocity.[53] The Maasai beadwork adorning sandals and baskets in Kariokor Market is another example. Maasai markets are also held in upmarket malls such as the Yaya Centre and the Village Market.

These examples of indigenisation affirm that African ethics, institutions and values did not all die off in the flood of modernisation, neoliberalism, digitisation and Chinese imports. Some have survived and are part of the contemporary African metropolis. Neo-traditionalists are trying to revive and reinstate African logic and ethics within urban culture (Kinyanjui 2012, 2014).

The protagonists who have actualised this cultural renaissance in Nairobi include clergy, traders, artisans, authors and intellectuals, many of whom have called for the decolonisation and (re)membering of African society. Urban planners, architects and economists have been slow to embrace this cultural renaissance but African logic, values and norms are gradually being entrenched in the city. Since their inception, Nairobi's marketplaces have been vibrant wellsprings of these values and norms. They are spaces in which African culture and business practices are consciously encouraged and transmitted. As I will show in later chapters, the entrepreneurialism practised by traders and artisans, which is based on solidarity and combines group agency with individual initiatives to gain entry to the urban economy, has proven more effective than any state policy in the Africanisation and indigenisation of Nairobi.

Exploring Nairobi's informal side

In every city, various class, cultural, historical, local, global, ordinary, elite and generational forces carve out their identity. In Nairobi, where little exists in the way of writings and memoirs, the names of places, neighbourhoods and businesses can tell us a lot about the identities, activities, values, meanings and aspirations of the people who live there. Place names also carry the memory and history of an area, of different regimes of accumulation and loss.

This is certainly true for Nairobi where a wide range of names describe and give identity to various aspects of the city. Some names are formally recognised while others are used informally by locals to express the value and meaning of the spaces or the activities carried out there. Many of the names given to residential estates that were built in the 1960s and 1970s (the first two decades after independence) express the aspirations of the time. Such names include Starehe, Umoja, Harambee, and Madaraka Estate.[54] Areas named Mwihoko (trust) and Wendani (love) signify different regimes of accumulation.[55] On the other hand, names such as Kosovo and Bosnia, given to slum localities, suggest the hardships residents face. Similarly, bus stops given names such as 'Kona Mbaya' (bad) warn commuters of the likelihood of muggings. Others, such as 'Civil Servant' in the Dandora area, describe the people who typically get on and off the bus at that point or who live in the surrounding streets.

These names are also revealing in the context of interactions between African, Western and East Asian cultures. Juxtaposed against Western and Oriental cultural forms, Africanness tends to be more fluid and ephemeral.

Without doubt, interaction between African, Western and Oriental cultural forms is evident in the formation of other African cities. Alfred Ndi (2007), for example, describes how labourers migrating from rural areas impact on West African cities by introducing indigenous practices. However, in my own earlier research (Kinyanjui 2012, 2014), I attempted to show that African logic and urban institutions are not necessarily contradictory or opposed to modernity. Instead, in some instances, they blend with the Western business ethos to create viable means of accessing markets and acquiring space in the city centres.

Although much urban theory remains silent or ambivalent about the role of African cultural forms in urbanism, many attempts have been made to 'rescue' traders and artisans or to 'revitalise' their dwelling places. Geared towards uprooting traders and artisans from their cultural environment and experiences, these initiatives often fail and sometimes leave people worse off. Such interventions seldom acknowledge the logic embedded in the ways that traders and artisans operate or bother to find out anything about the values and norms that they cherish. For example, in 2007, I facilitated a seminar on entrepreneurship for artisans. I was surprised when one of the participants expressed the need to ensure that the younger generation had access to quality education at school so that they would have other options besides working in a market. Since then, I have discovered that a good number of women traders in Nairobi define their success in terms of their ability to educate their children up to university level (see Kinyanjui 2014). What this helped me realise was that our needs and aspirations influence the way we negotiate our livelihoods, and our values and norms determine how we perform.

Nairobi's markets

Nairobi has 45 indigenous African markets. Several of these are located in large halls subdivided into stalls; others are comprised of separate cubicles arranged in rows. Over time, many of the markets have outgrown the space allocated, leading traders to occupy any available open spaces in the immediate surroundings.

Nairobi's oldest marketplaces are Burma and Kariokor. After Kenya achieved independence, new marketplaces were built as part of a strategy to address unemployment and provide places for new migrants and hawkers to work. The city council (now known as Nairobi County) owns the land on which most of these markets are located and rents the stalls to traders and artisans. In a few cases, traders and artisans own their own stalls.

Initially, most of the marketplaces were open-air and the construction of stalls and other infrastructure was forbidden. Traders were expected to bring their goods each morning and take them away every evening. Since moving goods is cumbersome, traders soon started leaving their wares behind in makeshift structures which could be used in the day to provide protection from the elements. The council routinely demolished these shelters raising tensions between the city council and the traders. In 1974, a delegation of traders and artisans met Jomo Kenyatta at his home in Gatundu and requested that roofed stalls be built from which they could trade. The president agreed and ordered that markets and stalls be constructed. This was actualised with the support of several Scandinavian countries. Traders were then allocated stalls for which they paid a fee to the council.

By building permanent structures in what had been open-air markets, the city legitimised the presence of traders and artisans for the first time. It also became a matter of city policy that marketplaces would be provided in all new residential estates in the city. Newer areas such as Githurai, Karen and Magiwa all have marketplaces. Since then, however, African markets in Nairobi have been neglected in terms of urban policy and planning. The marketplaces are unkempt and dilapidated. Little or no maintenance or development has taken place since they were first introduced. Despite this, traders have managed to maintain their foothold in the city through grit, solidarity and entrepreneurship, building their own networks to facilitate their entry and access to trade.

The traders' own resilience has been a major factor in the survival of the markets and the concentration of labour and capital that they represent. This has, in turn, contributed substantially to the evolution of the city. The markets enable workers in the public and private sectors, such as clerks, security guards, domestic workers, cleaners, waiters, hairdressers, shop attendants, factory workers, drivers, teachers, care givers, traders, and so on, to access a range of goods and services that would otherwise be unaffordable or difficult to obtain.

Prag (2010) coined the term 'nests' to describe marketplaces he studied. The term can usefully be applied to those in Nairobi as well, as it conveys something of how traders and artisans plan, hatch and nurture new businesses, while raising the capital that facilitates their claim to urban citizenship. The nests contain and sustain traders and artisans in urban spaces, providing work for some while allowing others to invest in urban housing and land. From within these nests, traders and artisans engage in competitive and collaborative politics, while the impact they make, and the culture they sustain, feeds into the city and beyond.

The role of markets in job creation and migration

Nairobi's markets are the spatial manifestation of traders' and artisans' drive and vision. The nests they create determine many of the relationships they form and how long they stay in business. They enhance traders' interdependence and encourage them to help their children or siblings to achieve more than they have. Their efforts to maintain their communities enhance their own agency and work to sustain not only the market but Nairobi's and, to some extent, Kenya's economy as well.

The ability to create jobs is a significant aspect of Nairobi's markets. As a result, the markets grow and new products are introduced. Naturally, this impacts on the evolution of the city as a whole. In general, migration patterns shift as people move to where they can find work, and the nature and quality of available work becomes an overall indictor of the quality of urban life. Where jobs are precarious, urban lifestyles will be poor. This in turn affects housing and consumption patterns as well as the supply of other services in the city. All these factors combine to shape the ways in which cities evolve.

An interesting development among Nairobi's traders and artisans is the hiring of labour. In capitalist enterprises, workers' wages are generally determined by their level of education – the higher the certificate, the higher the pay. In African tradition, if people work together on a project, any benefits that accrue are equally shared. According to King (1996), this tradition continues in Kenya's matatu industry and among jua kali collectives, which are groups of artisans that produce a range of metal products.[56]

In our study, 155 (55.2%) of the artisans surveyed employed others. Very few indicated that they pay a monthly wage to people they employ. Instead, they pay a fee per task, and have workers carry out specialised tasks such as measuring, cutting, folding, welding or painting. According to the secretary of Kamukunji Jua Kali Association,

> In jua kali, most of the work done passes through many hands. Manufacturing a wheelbarrow involves somebody fetching raw materials from the hardware shop [and bringing this] to where the artisan is. Since the wheelbarrow is composed of many parts, its parts are produced by different people. The work of the tyre of the wheelbarrow is subcontracted to someone who earns a commission while its bowl or container is marked and cut by another artisan. Fitting and assembling is given to a welder who is charged with the work of monitoring the whole job of assembling. After all parts have been assembled, the final work is given to a painter. After this, the item is taken to the market. Specific tasks are done by different workers. (Interview 2015)

Some traders and artisans are thus also employers (see Table 3 for additional survey data on employment practices).

Of the workers interviewed, most were recent migrants and lived in slums and other low-income neighbourhoods. The relatively low numbers of traders who said they employ people who live in their own residential area imply that economic informality is contributing to the evolution of lower-income areas. It could also be argued that the fact that employers and employees live in different areas might be creating two communities that are polarised in terms of income levels, which might eventually evolve into stratified classes of owners and workers.

In reality, however, these artisans and traders have not shed the principle of compensation whereby workers and the owners share the proceeds of their labour in equitable ways. In most instances, workers are paid according to the number of products they make. In other instances, workers receive a commission on sales in addition to a basic wage. Thus, unlike in the formal sector, workers in economic informality are compensated on the basis of their output. As one worker we interviewed put it,

> If I am paid on a monthly basis and during a particular month there is no work, the owner experiences a loss. However, if there is a lot of work and I am paid on a monthly basis I do not gain from the boom. The owner gains from the boom but I do not gain. To ensure we both gain, payment here is based on the number of products one makes. This also explains why some workers are able to transit to become business owners because of the savings they make during boom time. (Interview 2015)

If this mode of remuneration practice were to be extended and mainstreamed, it would undoubtedly create more economic equality.

TABLE 3 Survey results on employment practices by traders and artisans in Nairobi, 2015

Employment practices	Traders	Artisans
Number of businesses that employ workers	127 (33.7%)	155 (55.7%)
Number of workers employed	1–11	1–10
Number of female workers employed	1–5	1–6
Number of male workers employed	1–23	1–24
Duration of employment	1–24 years	1–18 years
Number of workers who become self-employed at the market after being employed by a trader or artisan	83 (72.2%)	132 (89.8%)
Number of employees trained by their employers	No data	69 (54.8%)
Number who employ relatives	30 (25.2%)	20 (13.2%)
Number who employ people from their own tribe	61 (51.3%)	58 (38.9%)
Number who employ people from their own faith	16 (13.6%)	15 (10.1%)
Number who employ people from their own residential area	24 (20.3%)	28 (18.4%)
Number who employ people of their own age	21 (16.7%)	27 (16.1%)

This information suggests that economic informality is creating a class of workers in Nairobi who might follow a different path to self-reproduction than the traders and artisans they work for, who own the means of production. This class of workers is comprised of both females and males who are recent migrants and slum dwellers. The majority have some secondary education and learn their trade through on-the-job training. Some share family ties with their employers but not always. Some traders and artisans hire workers from ethnic groups other than their own. This is interesting because it means that the communities are becoming more cosmopolitan, and this too will have significant implications for the evolution of the city.

Conflicts with planners notwithstanding, Nairobi's traders and artisans have contributed much to the evolution of Nairobi by creating a labour pool in and around the markets. Relations between market workers and employers are creating communities that are organised in non-hierarchical ways. Employers are not seen as bosses or workers as servants. Instead, each acknowledges their need for the other in ensuring the survival of the marketplace.

To sum up, it is time to rethink, reconstruct and redefine the notion of informality in ways that enable African business owners to engage effectively with global economic trends. The energies and loyalties nested in Africa's urban communities need to be tapped into as a source of economic dynamism. In the next chapter I highlight some of the key elements of those energies and loyalties and show how they contribute to shaping space in Nairobi.

Chapter 6

The 'African metropolis' in Nairobi

A plethora of literature exists on the disenfranchisement of workers in economic informality in African cities. For example, UN-Habitat (2010) holds the view that urban planning generally excludes the poor, while Watson (2009) shows how the development of master plans excludes economic informality in Africa. Caroline Skinner (2009), citing the case of Warwick Junction in Durban, demonstrates how traders are excluded from urban citizenship by the city's planning policies and its imaginaries of malls and municipal buildings.

When planners do take economic informality into account, they often seem inclined to control and eradicate it. For example, in the mid-2000s, Zimbabwean authorities infamously carried out a 'clean and restore order' in the country's urban areas by forcibly clearing slums and harassing, evicting and arresting what they termed 'illegal' traders (Kamete 2007). However, less has been written about *why* economic informality is so often excluded from modernist city spaces.

In this chapter, I describe how traders and artisans have resisted exclusion and asserted their citizenship rights to shape the environments in which they live and work.

Traders, artisans and participatory urban citizenship

In modern African cities, and in Nairobi in particular, traders and artisans have largely been excluded from urban citizenship. Most of the urban poor in Kenya have completed a basic Western education but are excluded from joining the elites by the fact that entrance examinations for both primary school and high school are difficult and pupils from lower-income areas are poorly prepared. Anyone unable to access formal work in domestic or multinational firms or in government services is deemed unqualified for modernity.

Historically, Nairobi's traders and artisans have not responded in subservient ways. As described in earlier chapters, they have fought both colonial and postcolonial governments for space and recognition, waging a formidable fight to claim space and gain legitimacy in the city. Their struggle has combined strategic, tactical and ideological resistance to, as well as compliance with, the city's rules and regulations. Through their presence, work and investment of surplus, they are engaged in a concerted process of creating an economic basis for their citizenship in the city. And while joining the global urban network, they draw from African logic, norms, values, personal experience and experience garnered via their social and business relations with others.

Achieving citizenship

Literature on the efforts of grassroots organisations to confer urban citizenship rights on people from lower-income communities is growing. For example, organisations in Nairobi such as Muungano wa Wana Vijiji and the Pamoja Trust are working to provide housing for the urban poor. In South Africa, Miraftab (2009) describes the Western Cape Anti-Eviction Campaign as an example of both urban insurgency and a radical planning initiative. Watson and Agbola (2013) outline planning initiatives between Makerere University's planning studio and the National Slum Dwellers Federation of Uganda to decolonise planning and open it to wider participatory processes. In India, Appadurai (2002) explains how an alliance of three civic organisations, the Society for the Promotion of Area Resource Centers (SPARC), the National Slum Dwellers Federation and Mahila Milan (a women's saving cooperative), secured land tenure, adequate housing and access to infrastructure. Such efforts, as Lyons and Brown (2007) observe, remain geared towards housing issues; what is still needed are political institutions that are willing and capable of supporting grassroots economic actors such as traders and artisans.

De Soto (1989) argues that informal workers have failed to become true capitalists *because* they are denied property rights. The denial of property rights affects their engagement in production, consumption and the disposal of surplus. He therefore recommends awarding property rights to the poor so that their 'dead capital' can be transformed into investment.

Notwithstanding the challenges and obstacles they face, Nairobi's traders and artisans have become part of the urban landscape. One indicator of this is their ability to meet their own consumption requirements in terms of food, clothing, health, children's education and shelter. Our survey revealed that few depend on welfare. Some 308 (83.5%) traders and 232 (82.3%) artisans surveyed said they were able to meet their own needs in urban areas and in the rural areas.

Furthermore, the survey revealed that, having met their basic needs, traders and artisans use their surplus to buy parcels of land and to build houses in both rural and urban areas. In other words, traders and artisans contribute to the formation of territorial complexes through investing and disposing of their surpluses where they live.

Owning or renting a residence in the city is one means by which we claim urban citizenship rights. Traders and artisans live in and dispose of their surplus income in the African metropolis. The African metropolis is different from the rest of the city due to the nature of the built environment *and* the social relations that shape it. The African metropolis is made up of slums, urbanised villages and self-developed urban fringes. Table 4 shows where the traders surveyed said they were living. Although a significant percentage of both traders and artisans were living in slums, almost the same proportion were living in the self-developed urban fringes – mainly in Githurai, Kasarani, Ruai and Kamulu. Regardless of where they were living, over 83% of traders and 82% of artisans said they were adequately meeting their own consumption needs at the time of the survey.

TABLE 4 Traders' and artisans' residential choices, Nairobi 2015

Living area	Traders		Artisans	
	n	%	n	%
Slum	154	40.0	97	33.6
Urbanised village	71	18.4	No data	17.3
Self-developed area on the urban fringe	150	39.0	132	45.7

Accumulating and allocating surplus income

Data from the survey show that Nairobi's traders and artisans still see themselves as following the African cultural tradition of conserving resources for future use. This practice now takes a variety of forms, including buying a cow, buying a goat, contributing to a social group, nurturing offspring and taking care of elderly parents. Resources are also conserved for emergencies and future needs such as initiation, marriage and death rituals. For a significant proportion, however, it now also includes buying a parcel of land, building a business space or buying transport (see Table 5). These statistics are important in legitimising their urban citizenship and sense of belonging to the city.

TABLE 5 How traders and artisans in Nairobi invest their surplus income, 2015

Mode of investment	Traders		Artisans	
	n	%	n	%
Building houses in Nairobi	76	21	67	24
Purchasing land in Nairobi or other towns	106	29	95	33
Building houses in rural areas/place of family origin	84	23	107	37
Purchasing own transport and pushcarts	93	25	69	24

Of the survey respondents, just under a quarter had invested in building houses in Nairobi itself. These buildings are situated in slums, urbanised villages or on the self-developed urban fringes. About a third of the traders had bought one or more plots in the city. Plots are considered an important asset because they rapidly appreciate in price and can be disposed of easily in case of a business or personal emergency. These respondents indicated that their plots were situated on the urban fringes, in areas such as Ruaraka, Mlolongo, Githurai, Syokimau, Kabete, Kangemi, Kamulu, Ruai, Kitengela, Mwihoko, Rongai and Ngong. Some had also invested in plots in other towns or cities, including Juja, Kikuyu, Kisii, Kiambu, Machakos, Murang'a, Nakuru and Thika.

Some 107 (37%) of the artisans and 84 (22.8%) of the traders surveyed had used their surplus to construct houses in other parts of Kenya such as Bungoma, Homa Bay, Kisumu, Kiambu, Murang'a, Machakos, Kitale, Makueni, Nyamira, Siaya, Meru, Kirinyaga and Nyeri. This might well be in line with the cultural logic that a migrant's ancestral home remains a key part of their identity. However, by investing in land and houses in Nairobi as well as in other cities and towns, traders and artisans are making territorial claims and laying down permanent footprints within the African metropolis. That is, they are changing the built environment and the provision of infrastructure. Their permanence in the city is changing the dynamics and the balance of power in the built environment as well as the political and cultural life of the city.

For urban planners and policy-makers, these data should shatter the stereotype of informal traders as 'temporary', 'survivalist' and 'marginalised'. This should open a path for planning to be done in inclusive and participatory ways rather than by imposing a textbook-based imaginary of what a city should be. City planners should work with the traders and artisans to design a city that allows for and encompasses their cultural logic, norms and values.

The data also revealed that approximately a quarter of traders and artisans had invested in means of transport such as boda boda taxis and pushcarts. These were used both to transport their own goods but also to earn additional income from transporting goods or people for cash. This diversification can also be seen as reflecting their efforts to claim a sense of belonging in the city.

The traders' and artisans' cultural logic of self-provisioning, their desire for independence, and their discretion in deciding how to allocate their surplus income all influence their place in the city. It can be argued that they are positioning themselves strategically in spaces that they feel will accommodate them – namely, higher-income parts of the city that are not Western or Asian in character. They are claiming territory in the slums, urban villages and the self-developed urban fringes. By living and investing in these spaces, traders and artisans are legitimising their presence in the city and contributing to the evolution of the African metropolis.

The logic of urban development planning in Nairobi has always been to modernise. In the contemporary era, this means creating a digitally connected and sustainable city. Competing with this mindset are traders, artisans and others who are struggling to create their own urban space based on African norms, values and logic. To help tackle the challenges they face when negotiating their livelihoods in the city, they are fashioning an African form of urbanism that honours African norms and values in human interactions as well as in architectural place-making and in the adoption of various technologies. I refer to the resulting urban forms as the African metropolis.

In the development discourse, this metropolis is often associated with overcrowding, crime and poverty (see UN-Habitat 2010). Urban theorists refer to such spaces as informal or unplanned and use them to differentiate the African cities from world-class megacities (Robinson 2002; Roy, 2007, 2011). Roy (2011) defines such spaces as zones of exception and Yiftachel (2009) describes them as 'grey cities'. I refer to them as African metropolises because they are distinctly different to Western and Asian models in terms of architecture, how human relations and transactions are fostered and the kinds of social innovations that are developed to address personal and urban challenges. These spaces include slums, urbanised villages, self-developed urban fringes and the African markets (see Plate 1).

In an attempt to imitate the African homestead that allows space for living, working, learning, leisure and interacting with close relatives, buildings of all shapes and sizes are constructed in the African metropolis. Rooms are created in the image of an African hut while additional rooms are added to existing single units in the compounds. The added units are used for work or for occupation by members of the extended family. The built environment in Nairobi's African metropolis exhibits the 'triple heritage' described by Ali Mazrui (1986) and the world evoked by Mugo Gatheru in his autobiography, *Child of Two Worlds* (1966).

Slums or ghettos

Slums are generally viewed as problematic, and it is certainly true that crime, dirt, hardship, poverty, insurgency, suffering, disease, displacement and dispossession are hallmarks of slums in Africa. Postcolonial urban discourse and practice has problematised and demonised these spaces but none of the solutions proposed so far has transformed them. Their persistence caused one urban thinker, Mike Davis, to claim that the earth is becoming a planet of slums. In his book *Planet of Slums* (2004), Davis describes slums as a 21st-century human catastrophe that represents the global community's inability to solve humanity's problems in megacities. UN-Habitat's (2010) report also laments the state of African cities in the new millennium and calls for action to save them. However, as Roy (2013: 142) observes,

> the slum is inadequate shorthand for the sheer heterogeneity of urban political economy: the diversity of informal and para-legal property arrangements, the dense economies of work and livelihood, and the complex formations of associational life and popular politics...If we recognize the slum not as defective or deviant, but rather as integral to the logic of urbanization, then of course it becomes evident that the slum, despite its inadequate nomenclature, signifies the global urban future of the world's urban majority.

In this chapter, I build on Roy's suggestion that slums are integral to the logic of urbanisation. I argue that the slums of Nairobi represent, first and foremost, the efforts of ordinary Kenyans to claim space in the city. The slums were where traders, artisans, domestic workers and other casual workers who were excluded from the city by colonial and post-independence housing policies made space for themselves in the city. They introduced African architecture to the city by building mud houses, and now use a range of materials including wood, corrugated-iron sheets and stone (see Plates).

The use of different building materials reflects the trajectory of slum development, showing the shift from mud to stone to corrugated-iron sheeting. These different materials demonstrate continuity and change in Nairobi's built environment. They also indicate that those investing in the slums are sensitive to the changes in the city's skyline – as the skyline changes elsewhere, it changes in the slums too.

But why do slums persist and evolve? Claudio Torres, a UN-Habitat consultant who has worked in Mathare slum in Nairobi, views the slum as indicative of the stage of industrial capitalist development that Kenya has reached and sees the slums as housing the cheap labour that supports capitalist industrial expansion in the city. Torres argues that the industrial revolution in Europe could not have happened without slums and that contemporary discourse on 'Africa rising' hinges on the fact that Africa's vast slum areas offer cheap labour to emerging industrial capitalist ventures (Interview 2015).

In my view, slums function as nests. They offer nurturing spaces for individuals who are envisioning a better life for themselves in the city or in the rural areas they are from. They are spaces in which everyday practices and transactions can occur in transient and temporary ways. Several features of slum life derive from African logic, norms and values. These include a culture of pragmatism, humaneness, solidarity and connectedness, and an ability to tolerate transient and temporal habitats. Survival in a slum is based on pragmatism and practicability, as illustrated by the stories of trader Edith Muhindi and student Jack Nyalando, who both lived in the slum of Mathare as they transitioned into the city. Edith recounts her story as follows:

> My mother broke up with my father in the village. She moved with four of us to my grandparents' residence. One night, she informed me that she was going to look for work. She left without

informing my grandfather. My grandfather moved us to another house where our aunt took care of us. My mother moved to Nairobi and was housed by an aunt who enrolled her in a tailoring school. When she finished the sewing course, she was employed as a tailor in a kiosk near Kiboro primary school. She settled in the slum, married someone else and took us to live with her.

She made clothes for women supporters of Ndururu Kiboro's political campaign for a seat in the county assembly. Kiboro was so impressed by her work that he gave her a parcel of land. She built a home consisting of three rooms, two for use by her family and one for renting out. She would purchase second-hand trousers from Asians, convert these into skirts for children, and give them to someone to sell in the slum.

My mother's new husband was an elder who was involved in allocating plots in the city and he had two water points where water was sold. I would work at the water point while my mother made clothes. I was assigned one of the water points. From its proceeds, my school fees were paid. The proceeds from my mother's water point were used for daily food and household supplies. Life was about trial and error. When things looked good, we started a timber and wood selling business but it stalled because my stepfather would draw money from it and use the money to drink alcohol. After the timber business went bust, my mother started meat and vegetable sales, an enterprise she did until she left the slum in 2002.

Always pragmatic and practical, she sold margarine in amounts small enough to cover a single slice of bread. Maize flour was sold by weight, making it possible to buy just enough for a single meal. Cooking oil was also sold in quantities just large enough to cook a single pot of food. The procurement of groceries for meals is made per meal rather than in bulk. This is based on the African logic of kumatha (harvesting or procuring enough food for a meal each day). Quantities are tailor-made to meet customer demand.

Edith's story illustrates that slums can be spaces where people go to seek solutions to problems they have in other spaces. Her example is typical of how decisions about living in the city arise as part of everyday solutions to personal challenges. Customers make choices based on existing cultural practices and continue to use resources in pragmatic and practical ways. Traders and artisans devise practical solutions to meet customers' demands. Trust is key, and credit is extended to regular customers experiencing hard times. However, by ensuring that consumption habits sustain life at the basic minimum, both sides reduce the risks involved in extending or accepting credit.

Slums are spaces of frugal living where individuals forgo today's comfort in the hope of securing comfort in future, and especially for children. Slums are where future urban generations are nurtured, who later seek or build other places to live for themselves and their parents. Edith's story is echoed in *Machachari*, a popular series aired by Kenya's Citizen TV channel. In the series, a character called Mama Baha is seen making efforts to nurture her children and negotiate her livelihood as a trader in a slum. She values education and is keen to ensure that her children receive a good one. She is also a strict disciplinarian. At one point she takes her children to her rural home for a holiday. *Machachari* highlights the nesting function of the African metropolis. The series also depicts the transience and temporality of slum settlements. All along, Mama Baha knows that one day she or her children will attain a better life and move to a different part of the city. Similarly, Edith informed me that several families she knows have moved out of Mathare but retain houses there.

According to Edith, Mathare was created by those who never had places in the city's designated African quarters – a place for security guards, retired housekeepers, traders and artisans. After finishing school, Edith found work and moved herself and her family to Githurai. She described the slum as a nest for the nurturing of creativity, noting that many Kenyan television personalities once lived there.

Edith's story also reveals that the slum is a space where people go to seek solutions and connection. Her mother survived because of her connectedness to other traders and artisans. In this sense, the slum is an extension of village life in the city. Essentially, Edith's story shows that the slums are spaces that nurture people as they make transitions into and around the African metropolis.

A culture of pragmatism and practicality influences the nature of any built environment. The logic in a slum is, 'If we do not belong and are here temporarily, why should we invest in upgrading the neighbourhood?' In African tradition, too, poverty is seen as a temporary phenomenon that individuals can overcome. Unfortunately, modernisation has made poverty permanent for many, keeping exit options accessible to only a tiny minority of poor people.[57] In this context, the slums continue to spread.

However, slums are also spaces where the traditional African values of solidarity and connectedness are enacted. To fulfil their duties of generosity, sharing and reciprocity, relatives invite family members to live with them in the slums. In this way, family and ethnic bonds have played a critical role in the creation and evolution of Nairobi's slums. Benjamin Obegi tells the story of Jack Nyalando, a medical student at Jomo Kenyatta University who started a clinic in his village in Western Kenya in 2013.[58] While he was still a child, Nyalando's father died and his mother was sickly. His aunt stepped in and invited him to Nairobi to pursue an education. She was a fishmonger in Mathare, and she enrolled him in a nearby primary school. He performed well at school and qualified for university. While attending Jomo Kenyatta University, he located an empty building near his village and turned it into a maternity clinic.

Nyalando's story demonstrates the role that family ties can play in the construction of slum life. Many people, like Nyalando's aunt, invite relatives to come to the city even if it means they have to live in the slums, because conditions in the city are perceived to offer better options. Undoubtedly, these invitations further the spreading and sprawling of slums. However, this is not necessarily negative. In this case, Nyalando's aunt used the surplus from her fish business to educate her nephew, and he in turn used his new knowledge and resources to establish a maternity clinic in his village.

Nyalando is quoted in the story as advising youth with opportunities to think about their communities, observing that 'in life everyone gets an opportunity to change their community'. His words provide some insight into the interdependence between the slum and the village, showing how social bonds work to build slum life and how individuals can be nurtured in the slums. His story also illustrates the reality that, after realising their goals, many slum dwellers move on to invest their energy and resources in solving problems elsewhere. That is, slums are seldom anyone's first choice when deciding where they want to invest any surplus they might accumulate. In fact, a slum is probably the last place where anyone would consider investing their surplus or using their knowledge resources to change slum life.

Instead, transactions and everyday interactions between people living in slums tend to be based on humaneness and solidarity. For example, when people move out of a slum, they generally leave their shack in place for a relative or someone from their village of origin to use. Individuals who live in slums show a high degree of connectedness with different territories in the national and urban space economy. For example, a person living in upmarket Woodley Estate is highly likely to have relatives in Kibera.

Urbanised villages

Nairobi's urbanised villages include settlements that are older than Nairobi, and that were the sites first occupied by the British. They include Dagoretti, Riruta, Kawangware, Kabete, Kangemi, Uthiru and Kinoo. As far as I am aware, no research has yet been published on the development and evolution of these settlements, but they seem to have largely resisted being incorporated into urban settlements, choosing to adapt at their own pace.

What is well known is that the British colonialists first constructed Fort Smith. Soon afterwards, missionaries such as the White Fathers moved into the Muthangari area and the Rev. Harry Leakey and his wife established a missionary school in Lower Kabete.

Dagoretti is said to be a Maasai name but some suggest it is a corruption of the word *ndagurite* which means 'the Europeans took land without buying it'. The word was apparently coined by women who resisted white occupation by refusing to allow the Europeans to collect firewood in the area because they had not bought the land. Stories of Agikuyu resistance note that the colonial administration was moved away from Fort Smith to the then unsettled plains now occupied by Nairobi's CBD because the Agikuyu community planted spikes on footpaths and frequently attacked Forth Smith.[59] As the city of Nairobi grew, African residents built houses for urban workers and attempted to preserve the logic of village life, honouring Mugumo sites of worship and creating a built environment that accommodated small-scale farming.

In 1969, Dagoretti was hived off from Kiambu district and was incorporated into the city boundaries by presidential decree. However, the area received no added infrastructural support and little practical urban development. The only notable council development was the building of the Dagoretti and Kangemi markets. Roads, water and lighting are poor. Individuals have been developing the compounds depending on their ability. The built environment contains both affluence and slums. Those who can afford it have buildings of stone; the rest build with iron sheets. In this way, the urbanised villages include those living on the margins even though most have been residents of the area since birth.

As small-scale agriculture is no longer viable here, most people engage in trade and artisan work and small real-estate developments. The traders mainly deal in foodstuffs, hardware and clothing; artisans do metalwork, carpentry and dressmaking.

It is common for structures in this area to contain several floors that are used for different activities including sleeping, cooking, working, relaxing and small-scale animal husbandry. Rooftops are often set aside as courtyards or shared spaces for relaxing, holding ceremonies, hanging out laundry and keeping goats and chickens. The second and third floors are often rented out to earn some extra income. The ground floor is where artisans work or traders sell their goods. Having several floors ensures that no family lives in isolation and structures can contain several generations. These buildings express the community's culture, work and sources of livelihood. The owners have brought the concept of keeping animals combined with other activities into the built environment.

Self-developed urban fringes

What I term the 'self-developed urban fringes' are situated outside old Nairobi's city boundaries. These extend northwards as far as Muthaiga to Westlands and down to Lavington in the south. They include areas to the north of the urban edge, including Zimmerman, Ngumba, Githurai, Kahawa Wendani, Mwihoko, Kahawa Jua Kali, Kahawa Sukari, Ruai and Kamulu. Two types of self-developed urban fringe environments are evident in Nairobi: controlled and uncontrolled.

The uncontrolled ones tend to include and accommodate people from all classes – people who earn low, middle and high incomes live side by side. What they have in common is a legal title to their land, which takes the form of an allotment letter, a share certificate or a title deed. No rules or regulations govern the designs or colours of their houses. Instead, homes are built according to the resources, skills, logic, norms and values of the owners.

Current thinking – as epitomised by UN-Habitat (2010) – attributes uncontrolled development of built environments to a lack of finances but in my view a lack of money has less impact than individual land owners' sources of creative inspiration and expression. Most owners build houses for their own occupation but some add extensions that they rent out. Some are inspired by African tradition, norms and values while others seem to be driven simply by greed. No coordinating body reviews the building plans, sizes or safety levels of structures as these areas are developing faster than the city's administration can handle.

Investors inspired by African traditions tend to value the idea of living, working, generating income, performing rituals and talking politics all in the same compound. They create buildings of all shapes and sizes. Those who are more inspired by filling their pockets tend to flout city and community norms by adding on backyard dwellings, kiosks or livestock pens that they can rent out or otherwise profit from. They either bribe city planners and administrators to look the other way or count on the community's willingness to ignore the rules. Where individuals do try to stand up and champion the rule of law and planning regulations in these areas, they can expect to be threatened and targeted by unethical land owners.

As in most other parts of the city, traders and artisans are an important part of the uncontrolled self-developed urban fringes. They earn their living from all manner of activities – from selling traditional foods such as boiled maize and beans or fried fish to secondhand clothing and furniture, organising money transfers, running hair salons and barber shops, bicycle courier services, baby and child care, metalwork and vehicle repair shops, and so on.

In the more controlled developments, buildings are approved by the city authorities, residents associations or a corporate developer. Here the authorities or developers specify the type and number of units that may be built on parcels of land, then they build the infrastructure for water, sewage and electricity, lay and name the roads, and determine the colours that may be used to paint the roofs and walls of buildings. In essence, these associations or developers do what the city council should do.

In terms of crime, petty thieves and other criminals found in slums and some of the uncontrolled urbanised villages are replaced by a different class of gun-wielding thieves who hide behind high perimeter walls, but also by civil servants, accountants, lawyers, insurance and tax advisers who steal with their pens, using fraud and corruption.

Self-developed urban fringes are inspired by high degrees of modernity but also attempt to accommodate some African logic, values and norms, such as décor with African themes, indigenous trees, animal rearing and crop farming. Not all people in these spaces, however, subscribe to the idea of animal rearing, building of kiosks, construction of rental spaces and the welcoming of traders and artisans in the fringes, citing security reasons. Some self-developed urban fringes have perimeter walls and are protected by privately hired security guards.

The common thread in the slums, urbanised villages and self-developed urbanised villages is the self-provisioning and building of houses to suit one's own taste. Another common feature is the effect of African logic, norms and values in influencing the desire to create places where one can live, work, rest, worship and farm. Also of significance is that traders and artisans are important in the supply of services and goods such as beef, animal feeds, fruits, vegetables, potatoes, clothes, cement, pipes, steel wires and construction services. Many traders, artisans and their workers also live in the African metropolis. Some dispose of their surplus here. They buy parcels of land, construct rental houses or invest in animals or vehicles for transport. In short, the integration of home, trade and craft has overflowed into some of these areas from the traditional African markets.

Part Three
Utu-Ubuntu Enhancing Urban Resilience

Chaper 7

The utu-ubuntu business model

I spent my childhood and teenage years in the village of Ngethu in rural central Kenya, which exposed me to some of Africa's indigenous economic and business logic, as well as its norms and values. My paternal grandfather was a farmer while my grandmother combined farming with selling agricultural commodities in local markets. My parents combined farming with formal employment in the civil service. My mother, a teacher, carried out her teaching duties between eight o'clock in the morning and three o'clock in the afternoon, returning to work on the farm when she got home. My father did his office work on weekdays but tended to his farm work on Saturdays and during vacations. My parents therefore straddled the world of modernity and the indigenous African world.

In 1987, I settled in Nairobi and, true to my roots, I established a habit of going to the market every Saturday. I became intrigued by the way traders share space, price their goods, collaborate and compete, differentiate between their products, treat their customers, acquire their supplies and adapt to the constantly changing modern business environment. Their agency and resilience ignited my desire to study the markets – their structures, functions, philosophies, regulations, abilities to adapt to change and their implications for urbanism and urbanisation.

As an economic geographer and scholar of small enterprises, I have searched for a business model that resonates with the values I experienced in Ngethu – values of resilience, self-reliance, solidarity entrepreneurship, economic justice, communal responsibility and inclusiveness. So far, the only model I have found that begins to fit these criteria is that practised by traders and artisans who run marketplaces in Kenya. As explained earlier, I have named it the utu-ubuntu business model. 'Utu' is a Swahili word for the state of being human and acting humanely. Ubuntu is a philosophical concept from southern Africa that refers to the inextricable interconnections between all human beings (Tutu 1999). The value system embedded in the philosophies of utu and ubuntu holds that all human beings occupy a single moral universe and share a moral sensibility that makes them recognise their duty to each other. As Kenyan philosopher John S Mbiti explains in his influential work *African Religions and Philosophy*, this is the understanding that 'I am because you are, and because you are therefore I am' (1969: 108).[60]

Few would suggest that economics can be divorced from our humanity even if solidarity and collaboration are not exactly championed in the world's currently dominant economic systems. However, as Polanyi (1944) describes it, in the 19th century, 'the great transformation' driven by industrialisation led to the global economy becoming disengaged from social control. The supposedly self-regulating 'free' market forms the basis of capitalism's entrenched inequalities. In response to the failures of the capitalist economy, many have advocated for an economy that serves everyone as opposed to rewarding only a small elite (see Hart et al. 2010). In previously published work, I have that the ethics and practices of traders and artisans in African markets offer a tangible example of a more humane economic system (Kinyanjui 2012, 2014). This is a system in which values and norms, combined with an awareness of how our actions impact on others, determine the economic strategies we deploy (De Dora 2011).

The basics of utu-ubuntu business practice

The business logic that informs traders and artisans in African markets is about endurance, loyalty, sharing, hard work, concern for the welfare of others, resilience and generosity. I make this claim based on examples drawn from the Agikuyu community in central Kenya.

For as long as anyone can remember, the Agikuyu have engaged in the manufacturing and trade of art and craft. They set up manufacturing centres or craft collectives where carvers and blacksmiths congregated, and were adept not only at carving and forging, but also at weaving, dyeing, ceramics and leather working. They produced a wide range of metal goods (including knives, farm implements, jewellery, chains and musical instruments), leather goods, wooden objects, cloths and complex ceramic work. They engaged in trade and manufacturing to satisfy their need for food, clothing, shelter and security, exchanging goods through bartering at markets and via trade caravans.

Community cohesion in relation to socio-economic transactions was maintained through membership of *nyumba* (households) and *riika* (age groups). As everyone belongs to both an age group and a household, these bonds contain and link communities into a shared lineage. It is in the best interests of both individuals and the community to preserve unity and good relations at these levels. Egalitarianism is maintained by controlling inequalities and disparities that might breed acrimony between people who share a common ancestry. Individual initiatives, related to negotiating a livelihood or facing personal challenges, for example, are always seen as being connected into a frame of community activities and social relationships.

Economically, community-based activities are supported by solidarity and collaboration, which I have termed 'solidarity entrepreneurialism'. This is enabled and enhanced by accessing *ngwatio* (labour pools) and *matega* (resource pools) that exist within or are linked to household and age-mate communities. Its benefits are expressed by Mama Nguyai, a respondent from Kairi Village

115

as follows: '*Kunyitanira nokuo ngungituma andu mahote gukura. Gukura wi wi ka ti wega. Tondu mundu ndagiriirwo guikara nyoike ta mbogo ya nduiki. No muhaka wite ucio ungi munyitanire*' (Solidarity and collaboration is the only way that people can grow and live together in harmony). There is general acknowledgement that no one can live well in solitude, and they maintain group agency by recognising the strength that lies in unity.

Shared risks

Mwalimu Gacheru, a respondent from Nguna, offers the following advice: '*Mundu akihanda mwere ni eraga andu angi onao mahande nigetha ma gateithania nyoni*' (while planting 'mwere' [a type of grain], an individual invites others to do the same so that they would share the risk of the seeds being eaten by birds). In an urban context, traders share risk by inviting others to join their projects by sharing space, transport and security costs. They spread their risks by investing in similar businesses, thereby making collaboration more useful than competition. The general sense of not having to 'go it alone' encourages traders to stay in business.

Building individual agency

Sharing risks does not imply an absence of individual agency. Individuals are required to gather the willpower, capacity and skills to engage effectively in trade. Rather than using technologies to ease individuals' workloads, the Agikuyu community invests in building individuals' agency. Mostly, this involves enhancing people's skills and perseverance when embarking on economic activity – for example, *ngwatio,* a form of pooled labour that beefs up an individual's capacity to complete a particular task such as clearing bush from a piece of land. In an urban context, groups of construction workers use *ngwatio*, combining their energies to enhance their output and increase their bargaining power (Kinyanjui 2012). A similar example was provided by a respondent who noted, '*atumia nima nyitanaga magathii ndunyu hamwe nigetha momaniririe njira*' (women travel together to the market as a way of helping each other endure the long distances that have to be covered).

Similarly, individuals often pool their savings in a *chama* (cooperative), thereby enhancing their ability to afford certain kinds of transactions. In less formal ways, networks of friends, relatives and colleagues surround individuals with the social fabric within which they can strengthen their confidence to undertake economic actions. People transact economically, secure in the knowledge that they are both an individual and a member of the community. Being part of supportive networks and engaging collaboratively in work is seen as a way to guarantee thriving. The spirit of mutual reciprocity and trust built via shared effort also helps to ensure that transactions agreed to are fair.

Economic justice

In Agikuyu tradition, *ndunyu* (markets) and *iganda* (manufacturing sites) were where economic activity was carried out. Anyone was free to sell goods at a market and those with artisanal skills would sell their wares at manufacturing sites. Goods were bartered and relations between workers and employers were based on a reciprocal system of gifts and rewards that emphasised fairness. Importantly, all activities were carried out openly, which helped to minimise injustices such as hoarding, unfair trade terms, overpricing, undercutting and exploitation. The old adage *murimi ndaunagwo guoka* ('never break the hand of a farmworker'), is still widely quoted.

Savings and surpluses

Johnson (2012) describes savings behaviour in Kenya in a paper titled 'The rift revealed: The search for financial inclusion in Kenya and the missing social dimension'. She claims that Africans do not save, but rather store money in large sums and draw from this bit by bit. Johnson explains that villagers she spoke to conserved money for the future in what was known as *kuiga muthithu* (conserving in a chest). She also observed that villagers she got to know did not consume their entire harvest in one year. Nor did they take everything they had grown or made when they went to sell goods at the market. Instead, goods and produce were preserved for the longer term and in case of emergencies. Accordingly, every home had a granary for storing grain. Similarly, goats owned by one household were periodically sent to a neighbour's homestead for safe keeping. After some time, the goats would be returned with new offspring. In this way, communities preserved and shared their best breeding stock. Johnson argues that this kind of preserving and conserving is different from stockpiling goods for disposal via a stock exchange when prices are good.

To a large extent, similar norms, values and logic about sharing and conserving can be observed in African indigenous markets. The markets act as nests that contain the relational dynamics within which the production, exchange and conserving of surpluses take place. Traders often pool their resources to insure one another in a kind of crowd-funded group insurance. Labour and capital are organised around utu-ubuntu circles of family, friends, age-mates and ethnic ties.

Labour relations

In the indigenous economy, people worked collaboratively to grow crops, raise livestock and market their goods. At times, a gendered division of labour was clear. For example, men would cut sugar cane while women and children would carry the canes to the weighing bay. However, men, women and children all weeded maize and bean fields. In addition, communities pooled their labour in groups known as *ngwatio*, enabling neighbours to call on each other for additional help when necessary. They also pooled their resources in groups called *matega*, whereby neighbours shared seeds, cuttings and suckers.

Solidarity entrepreneurialism

This sharing of labour and resources is typical of what I see as the African business ethic, which foregrounds resilience, self-reliance and entrepreneurship, as much as solidarity, sharing risk, economic justice, building individual agency and conserving surpluses for the future. Business activities are seen as closely linked to, and embedded in, not just the life and work of any single individual, but also to the life of the community and to its relationship with the divine. That is, the links between these three spheres of life are understood as interdependent and they therefore frame a moral and ethical code that shapes relationships, business activities and the deployment of surplus.

This African business model has struggled to coexist with the capitalist ethos which reveres individualism and lauds those who survive as the fittest, the smartest and the most intelligent. Yet, on the fringes of the urban economy, the African model persists. It still insists on the logic of interdependence, self-reliance and community mindedness, and remains embedded in ethical norms and religious values. In earlier work (see Kinyanjui 2010, 2012, 2013, 2014), I observe that this same set of African logic, norms and values continues to drive the economic activities of traders and artisans in Nairobi's informal sector, and that their ways of working exemplify the solidarity entrepreneurialism that characterises the utu-ubuntu business model.

In my view, solidarity entrepreneurship is the key tenet of African business values and ethics. It comprises group agency and individual initiatives in which competitors aim to collaborate via collective alliances rather than attempting to destroy each other (Kinyanjui 2013, 2014). Solidarity entrepreneurialism among women garment traders in Nairobi sees entrepreneurs sharing spaces and transaction costs, deciding together on which risks to take and which to avoid, and inviting others to join them in their businesses. Every action is illuminated by a sense of solidarity, and this underpins the utu-ubuntu business model.

Figure 1 is a graphic representation of how individual traders seem to perceive their choices within this African economic form. Traders and artisans acknowledge that they live in a wider world of political turbulence and economic crisis. They operate at the mercy of stifling government policy and in the face of strong competition from formal businesses that are generally supported by state policy and thus have access to several sources of capital.

The utu-ubuntu philosophy encompasses both the business and wider lives of traders and artisans. Traders see themselves as

FIGURE 1 *Traders' and artisans' perceptions of their economic options in the globalised economy*

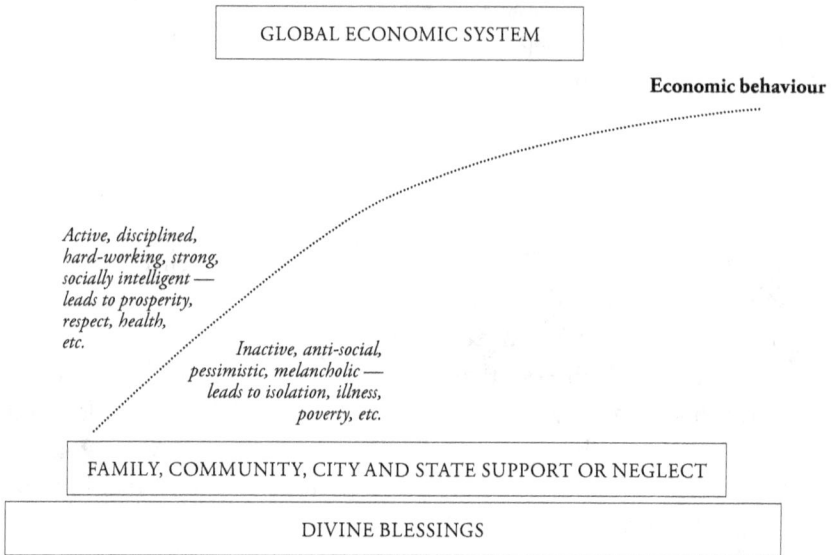

embedded in both the divine and physical worlds and the ideals and objectives of life, work and spirit are equally nurtured. In the marketplaces, the interplay between the social, economic and spiritual domains is always evident. No individual is really separable from the business nor the business from the household, and both exist within the grace of a higher power. This approach to the totality of life defines the nature of all transactions and activities.

The role of divine forces in traders' and artisans' economic activities should be understood within the context described by Mbiti (1969) who notes that Africans are notoriously religious. This religiosity is evident in the large numbers of Africans who proclaim or profess one religion or another. Most of the market traders and artisans I spoke to said that they often hold prayer meetings at the markets in the early mornings before the stalls open for business. Their belief that divine forces are in overall control provides traders and artisans with the confidence to engage in business and to accept its outcomes even when these are not immediately positive for them.

More mundane factors affecting traders' and artisans' economic behaviour include their family and community backgrounds. In the utu-ubuntu context, traders' and artisans' families usually provide the educational and monetary backing for new entrants to their businesses. Often, the wider community also offers support by providing ideas, finances, skills training and/or a base of loyal customers. The ability to invite new members into their businesses, and to train and support them initially, also serves as a yardstick for the success of families and communities, as the ability to share and be generous is an important social and economic indicator. In other words, business success is measured not only in terms of assets accumulated but also in terms of how people treat others and conduct themselves socially – how they take care of their children's education and their parents' welfare, the type of housing they choose and their contributions to church and community groups. Economic well-being is also judged by investments made in both urban and rural areas in terms of real estate, animal husbandry and forms of transport. Any event in the life of a household or business is shared and lived by the community as a whole.

In summary, the utu-ubuntu business model is characterised by its embeddedness in the personal, community and divine domains. It is driven by a spirit of solidarity as well as courage, endurance, resilience and hard work. Entrepreneurial behaviour is characterised by solidarity entrepreneurialism, which encourages individual initiatives in a context of group agency. Group agency is reflected in the sharing of transaction costs, such as transport, security and space rentals, learning from older traders and later mentoring new ones, agreeing to rules that regulate the group and pooling assets. Individuals are expected to work hard, live frugally and show determination, perseverance and a willingness to be self-reliant. This is the spirit of entrepreneurship that is nurtured and flourishes in African markets.

Chapter 8

Utu-ubuntu nests, bonds and associations

In a world where humanity is polarised on the basis of class, colour, ethnicity, gender, religion and technology, and threatened by the impact of rampant consumerism and global warming, we urgently need to consider how to build communities capable of harnessing human agency for planetary survival. Class-based struggles call for the dismantling of capitalism and the control of globalisation to help reduce inequality, but the collapse of communism left the world with few clear options in this regard. Neoliberal approaches that advocate modernisation and industrialisation via the introduction of free markets, the democratisation of political institutions and the adoption of universal human rights hold sway. Attempting to forge some kind of alternative, the BRICS alliance (consisting of Brazil, Russia, India, China and South Africa) seems to be attempting to use centralised state capitalism to power up its economies. Meanwhile, fundamentalist movements all over the world are engaging in a range of strategies, from violence to isolation, to preserve their community identities and challenge the dominant culture. Some of these have been led from the top by strong leaders while others have arisen from below.

In Africa, democratic transitions have been difficult to manage, especially with regard to the incorporation of minorities and the provision of services for poorer urban and rural communities, leaving many with no choice but to come up with their own strategies for inclusiveness. Given the tenuousness and fragility of life in African cities for those excluded from the formal economy, a host of social networks exist to help and support individuals. Imbued with the spirit of utu-ubuntu, these networks help people negotiate their lives and livelihoods. When individuals are sick or households are struck by calamity, these networks contain and reduce individuals' vulnerabilities; the same networks also provide support at happy times, such as childbirth, marriage and graduation parties (Kinyanjui 2010, 2012).

Traders and artisans create their own communities based on African norms, values and logic, adapting the utu-ubuntu model to the urban environment. In development discourse, their initiatives are often perceived as creating an 'eyesore', as examples of 'incomplete urbanisation' – survivalist, spontaneous, unpremeditated and as 'an indication of everything that is wrong with urbanisation'. In response, state officials and development workers tend to offer 'solutions' aimed at the provision of technical fixes such as credit facilities, entrepreneurial or organisational skills training and social protection. What traders and artisans actually need is for their worldview, dignity, freedom and right to space to be recognised so that their legitimate livelihood strategies are accommodated and affirmed in city planning models.

In the face of constant marginalisation, Nairobi's traders and artisans have chosen to harness the agency of their own communities in advancing their struggle for survival. In carving out the nests that serve as their workplaces, they have constructed territorial complexes that form the African metropolis in which they consume and live. In the nests, a division of labour between investors and workers reproduces a form of communal life that is governed by rules and regulations. Relations between the nests contribute to the evolution of the metropolis as surpluses are reinvested or redistributed. They also facilitate the flow of goods and services in the city. In addition, traders and artisans generate technical changes in production as they learn and innovate. To borrow a term used by Robinson (2013), the utu-ubuntu model can be theorised as a form of the 'urban now' in African cities. It also constitutes a visible urban form, as described by Jenkins (2014) and Myers (2011).

In this creative process of space making, the traders and artisans have drawn on logic, norms and principles of utu-ubuntu to set the parameters of what is perceived to be rational and ethical behaviour. That is, bonds of connectedness, as nurtured through family and kinship ties, as well as market traditions, rituals, social bonds and associations, form the basis of individual and community action and help ensure individuals' survival. A key question is whether these social bonds and associations play a developmental role in the lives of the individuals involved.

Anthropologists trace group behaviour from early human societies of gatherers and hunters. The evolution of individualism is seen by some as an advanced stage in human development. However, even in post-industrial societies, group behaviours prevail and alliances in business and politics remain a key aspect of social and economic action. In his book *Critical Mass*, Philip Ball (2004) observes that interaction matters because motion is central to any given mass. Atoms in any mass are always in motion. Traders and artisans, like atoms, are constantly in motion within Africa's urban spaces. From my observations, their movements, whether in abstract or physical space, are generally driven by a sense of solidarity with others as they try to solve everyday problems or celebrate everyday victories in their lives.

Appadurai searches for models to try to understand more of how the poor function in cities. In his article 'Deep democracy: Urban governmentality and the horizon of politics' (2002), he proposes that alliances form between the elites and the poor. These alliances tend to position the knowledge and capacities of the poor at the centre of urban politics, keeping poor people politically neutral while using their development needs to drive change. Appadurai suggests that through harnessing the deep democracy within such alliances, urban and development practitioners have the potential to find grassroots solutions to the problems of social inequalities in cities.

Nembhard (2014) demonstrates the role of collectives run by African Americans in the US economy from the days of slavery up to the present. Her studies highlight how communities formed cooperatives and connected with one another to achieve their objectives. In a similar way, traders and artisans in Nairobi are highly interconnected and driven by the need to survive. Their understanding and experience of survival is illuminated by their sense of the need to work in solidarity with others in the market spaces that I refer to as utu-ubuntu nests. The nests function as spaces for nurturing members' social, economic and spiritual goals. They are formed by groups that are united in purpose and intention, and that are also closely interconnected by family, friendship and ethnic ties.

Characteristics of utu-ubuntu nests

The operational behaviours and management structures that traders and artisans have created for these nests are multidimensional and multipurpose. They are multidimensional in the sense that they affect everyone involved the markets, many of the people in the extended networks within the African metropolis in which they live, as well as all the inhabitants of the rural towns and villages from which their families derive and in which they will probably eventually be buried. They are multipurpose in that they extend beyond business operations to encompass the social, health, educational and political concerns of traders and their families. For example, given that death is both inevitable and unpredictable, a revolving fund supports members when bereavement occurs. The intertwining of business and individual life experience differentiates the African market from other business or industrial districts and special economic zones.

It is easy to see that the ways in which traders and artisans in African markets collaborate in terms of production and exchange are different from the individualist and competitive behaviours prevalent in so-called free markets. Traders and artisans aim to maintain communities of production and exchange that enable members to harness their agency. As a result, everyday transactions in Nairobi's markets reveal how traders care for and maintain their communities. They share space, transport and security costs, pool savings and team up to make bulk purchases. As shown in Table 6, 67% of traders we interviewed reported collaborating with each other, and 80.2% of the artisans reported collaborating with other artisans. Over 90% of both traders and artisans reported supporting their colleagues in their social and personal endeavours. Some 74.5% of traders and 81.9% of artisans thought the market would collapse if they did not support each other, and over 80% felt responsible for maintaining a sense of community.

TABLE 6 *Perceptions of relationships among traders and artisans interviewed in Nairobi, 2015*

Perceptions reported	Traders		Artisans	
	n	%	n	%
I collaborate with other traders at work	255	67	231	80.2
I collaborate with other traders in social and personal endeavours	351	91.6	268	93.4
The market would collapse if traders and artisans did not support each other	286	74.5	235	81. 9
Traders and artisans are responsible for maintaining harmony in the marketplaces	314	82.8	238	82.6

Decision-making by consensus

Decisions that affect the group occur in small chats and in heated meetings. In 2015, I attended a meeting at Uhuru Market at which the idea of forming a market-wide savings and credit cooperative was proposed. Here the extent of the group's discursive and democratic nature was revealed. Each person was given time to express themselves until the importance of having a market-wide cooperative had been understood and accepted by everyone. All the merits and demerits of the idea were discussed to ensure that everyone was aware of all the issues. The amount of money to be saved was discussed and a figure that everyone could pay was calculated. The leadership struck me as extremely patient.[61]

Shared narratives and fables

In the absence of manuals and websites documenting sources of quality stock, raw materials, or technologies, narratives become trusted sources of information. Narratives enable individuals to process information, draw conclusions and learn lessons. Stories give listeners the freedom to choose a response. The narratives are based on life experiences and may be contemporary or handed down from the past. In Kamukunji Market, for example, the story of an artisan who lied to a customer about the whereabouts of another artisan is known to all the traders. The story goes that a customer wanted to buy a product from a certain artisan but the man was not present. An artisan in a neighbouring stall told the customer that the man he was looking for had long passed on. The customer then decided to buy the goods from this second man but before the transaction was concluded, the allegedly dead man returned to his stall. The artisan who had lied ran away in shame and could not complete the sale. The moral of the story is clear and it is often retold.

Traders and artisans use stories to share an epistemology about survival in urban spaces. What contributes to their survival in conditions of extreme hardship is their ability to maintain a narrative of hope that helps them stick together and celebrate their resilience. Artisans interviewed described their experiences in the markets as challenging but rewarding. Many said the market had given them productive lives that enabled them to make money and support their families. For others, the market had given them opportunities to 'hang in there'.

Keeping the community close

Although traders and artisans might seem to operate quite simply, they have distinct and complex systems that are difficult to deconstruct as they tend to be quite reserved when talking about themselves. In her short story, 'The Banana Eater', Monica Nyeko (2014) depicts market traders as a united force who strongly resist the order and aesthetics of modernity. They confront adversity together and they gossip and laugh often. Nyeko's depiction stands in stark contrast to the image of traders that features in much development and planning discourse. Planners and academics tend to perceive traders and artisans as individuals who have little vision and few plans for their lives; they are portrayed as illogical and disorganised, as acting with little economic, cultural or social logic and, therefore, as reliant on the elite to bring about change and give them some agency.

In reality, utu-ubuntu nests provide breeding grounds and nurturing frameworks for traders and artisans, providing space within which they can meet their basic needs, learn business skills, explore new opportunities, develop their talents, support their families and celebrate their culture.

The survey that formed part of this study confirmed that family and friends were important in introducing new traders to the markets. As shown in Table 7, of traders introduced to the markets by friends, 65% were from the same tribe and 28% were from the same school. Some 21% were introduced by people from the same religious community while 45% were introduced via friends living in the same estate. Several of the categories in the table overlap and respondents were encouraged to choose all options that applied to them, but it is interesting to note that 69% of traders noted that their friends were also their age-mates.

TABLE 7 *How respondents were introduced to markets in Nairobi*

Introduced by	Percentage
Friends from same tribe	65
Friends from same school	28
Members of the same religious community	21
People living in the same area	45
Age-mates	69

What this reveals is that markets constitute (and exist within) communities of people who are bound together by a range of interlocking ties of family, religion, residence, ethnicity, friendship and age group. These ties have a bearing on the nature of transactions carried out in the markets and make them spaces where traders are willing to act together in coordinated ways, from organising a funeral to resisting eviction.

Traders also support one another through major life events such as birth, death and disaster. For example, when Uhuru Market's Block D was gutted by fire in 2010, all the other blocks closed in solidarity. Members of the market fundraised and contributed to the construction of a new block of stalls. Bonds are further reinforced by goat-eating parties held by male traders to celebrate important events in their lives and by *chama* (informal cooperatives) group meetings organised by the women. Such gatherings also act to bind the traders and artisans together in ongoing ways, influencing their actions and enhancing their dedication to one another.

Common needs and goals

According to traders and artisans who responded to the survey, they join the market trade out of desire and need, perceived opportunities and innate talent or inclination. Most want to be self-employed and productive, and they need income. Perceived opportunities include the availability of customers and their experience of gaps in the market. Their talents include their skills and interest in learning to fulfil certain tasks. None of the respondents indicated that they had acted spontaneously or haphazardly when joining the market. They also stated that they would continue to work in the market until their desires and needs were fulfilled. In this, they deliberately join communities of people with similar interests who are willing to work together to realise their needs or maintain a family business. They have no reason to quit until their desires are fulfilled.

Shared knowledge and skills

Cognition and learning are important aspects of building resilience in relation to urban livelihoods. A quote I once saw on the back of a taxi on Nairobi's busy Thika Road said *mjini akili kijiji nguvu* (in cities cognition is required while in rural areas strength dominates). This reflects a perception common in Kenya of a dichotomy between rural and urban areas and of the different responses this demands from human beings: in cities, reasoning and learning are key while in rural areas, physical strength is vital.

As McFarlane (2011) points out, tacit knowledge is seldom explicitly acknowledged by urban theorists as an integral part of urbanisation and is neglected in understandings of urban politics and everyday survival strategies. In general, the problems that beset many cities are envisioned as resolvable through a gradual balancing of power relations such that institutions are increasingly democratised rather than through the sharing of learning processes that might enhance 'cityness' or urbanism. In this section, I delve into how utu-ubuntu commercial nests facilitate learning, and innovation among traders and artisans, as well as the types of knowledge transmitted and the methods used to transmit them.

Human survival in cities involves learning particular techniques of production and exchange while negotiating one's way through various sets of power and public relations. In Nairobi, the formal business sector is represented in the structures of city management. Informal traders have no such representation, and the power relations between them and the city authorities are extremely unequal. Nevertheless, traders and artisans have long begged and struggled for recognition and representation. In this process, they have had to learn to use and negotiate in language that city managers understand.

The traders have learned this language, and acquired the knowledge on which it is based, despite neglect and hostility from the city authorities. They have also had to overcome their own limitations, fears, uncertainties and limited literacy levels. Their acquisition of this knowledge has been a survival strategy, constructed and obtained outside of mainstream channels of formal education. They have had to decode and unpack the knowledge held by city managers and administrators and find means of surviving against the odds. They have accomplished much more than mere survival.

Urban planners, architects and city managers acquire their knowledge and hone their skills in schools, colleges and universities locally or abroad. Traders and artisans learn via experience in non-school environments and share their skills and knowledge informally within their social networks and among fellow traders. Having acquired knowledge from such very different sources, misunderstandings and even conflict between these groups should not be surprising. For example, in an earlier study (Kinyanjui 2010), I discuss a conflict between two groups of residents in Nairobi's Kahawa Sukari Estate. Drawing on the logic of village or rural survival, one of the groups wanted to keep farm animals in their city homesteads. The other group wanted the estate to be run purely along Western lines, allowing only dogs, cats and possibly horses.

In terms of daily living, survival for traders and artisans in Nairobi requires frugality and prudence. Basic costs for food, healthcare and shelter are kept to a minimum. This means living in the least expensive areas in the city and walking or using the cheapest means of transport. It also means learning which parts of the city are safe to walk in, which schools are suitable, which church to attend and which doctors are affordable. It means being able to identify opportunities and make the best of them. All this aggregated knowledge creates resilience.

Traders and artisans in markets mainly draw on tacit knowledge that develops through lived experience and is transmitted through family and friends. As shown in Table 8, gender and ethnicity also determine information flow to some extent. Interviews revealed that some traders had taught themselves through trial and error, but most had learned from friends, peers and family. Some had worked in the formal sector and acquired some useful skills. Mothers and husbands were the family members most frequently cited as trainers. A few mentioned learning skills at schools, polytechnics, colleges, traders' seminars or trade organisations. Among the artisans interviewed, knowledge transfer took place mainly through family with brothers, fathers and grandfathers being the most important family members offering training. Artisans also noted that their friends were important sources of knowledge while some said they were self-taught.

Knowledge transfer between traders and artisans covers many aspects that relate to business and the ways in which the market operates. Some of the technical skills include how to use weights and measures, how to display and price goods, as well as how and where to source reliable and affordable products or supplies. Good suppliers are key because they determine the quality and selling price of a commodity. Selling poor-quality or overpriced goods quickly ruins reputations. Budgeting for stock purchases, calculating profit margins and saving for investment are other key technical skills. Traders have to know how to set a price that will not undercut other traders but not be so high as to deter customers. Customer care is another crucial skill that involves learning to approach and communicate with customers in ways that make it likely that they will return. Quality control and cleanliness are crucial here.

TABLE 8 *Sources of training for traders and artisans interviewed in Nairobi, 2015*

Learning source	Traders		Artisans	
	n	%	*n*	%
Traders or artisans working at the same market	157	67.7	139	59.7
From somebody else as opposed to self-taught	231	61.6	No data	No data
People from their tribe	139	52.7	136	58.6
People they went to school with	33	12.5	21	9.1
People who live in same estate	99	38.1	40	17.2
Male traders or artisans	74	28.6	132	57.6
Female traders or artisans	72	27.8	No data	31
Both male and female traders or artisans	113	43.6	66	28.6
From younger traders and artisans	56	22.0	33	14.4
From older traders and artisans	85	33.3	118	51.5
From older and younger traders and artisans	114	44.7	78	34.1

Artisans learn a wide range of technical skills. Apart from the basics of their craft – joinery, tailoring, welding, carving, sewing, etc. – they also have to know about design, accuracy and quality control. They also need to keep up with consumer trends and changes in the market.

Continuous learning and skills transfer ensures that the artisan trades are preserved and passed on to the next generation. The fact that these skills are carefully passed on implies that traders do not leave their businesses to chance. They acquire knowledge through close observation and practice, and continually make calculated moves to sustain and improve their businesses.

Through the nature of their work and the context they work in, traders and artisans also learn to be resilient, patient and hardworking. They learn to work in solidarity with others even when they are competitors. They have to regulate their jealousies and self-interests. They learn social mechanisms to help them deal with personal and business challenges. These learning experiences increase both the sustainability of these entrepreneurs and their interdependence on each other.

The passing on of knowledge and skills strengthens traders' bonds with one another as they owe their presence and success in the market to their trainers and mentors. The transfer of knowledge from the older to the younger generation ensures a generational bond, as well as the continuity and survival of the market. By enhancing the bonds between the market traders and artisans, learning becomes a foundation for resilience. The importance of unity and bonding in the market is evident during the joint actions that occur when the municipality increases fees and when fire or other disasters affect a particular market. To a large extent, the pedagogy of survival and resilience that pervades African markets largely depends on the bonds of solidarity that traders and artisans continually build and maintain.

Plates

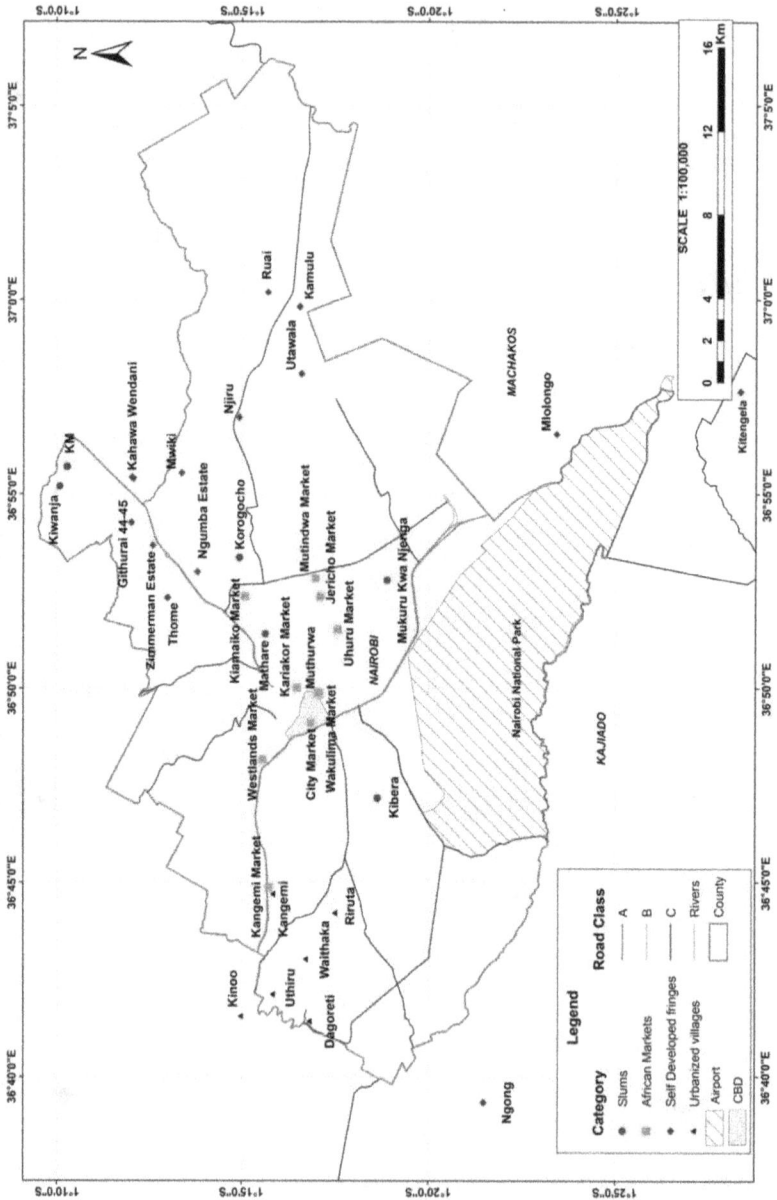

PLATE 1   Nairobi: An African metropolis

PLATE 2   *A bird's-eye view of the African metropolis*

PLATE 3   *An example of a slum settlement*

PLATE 4   *City council-controlled and -serviced urban space*

PLATE 5   Mixed trade and residential space in self-developed urban areas

PLATE 6 *An area typical of the self-developed urban fringes*

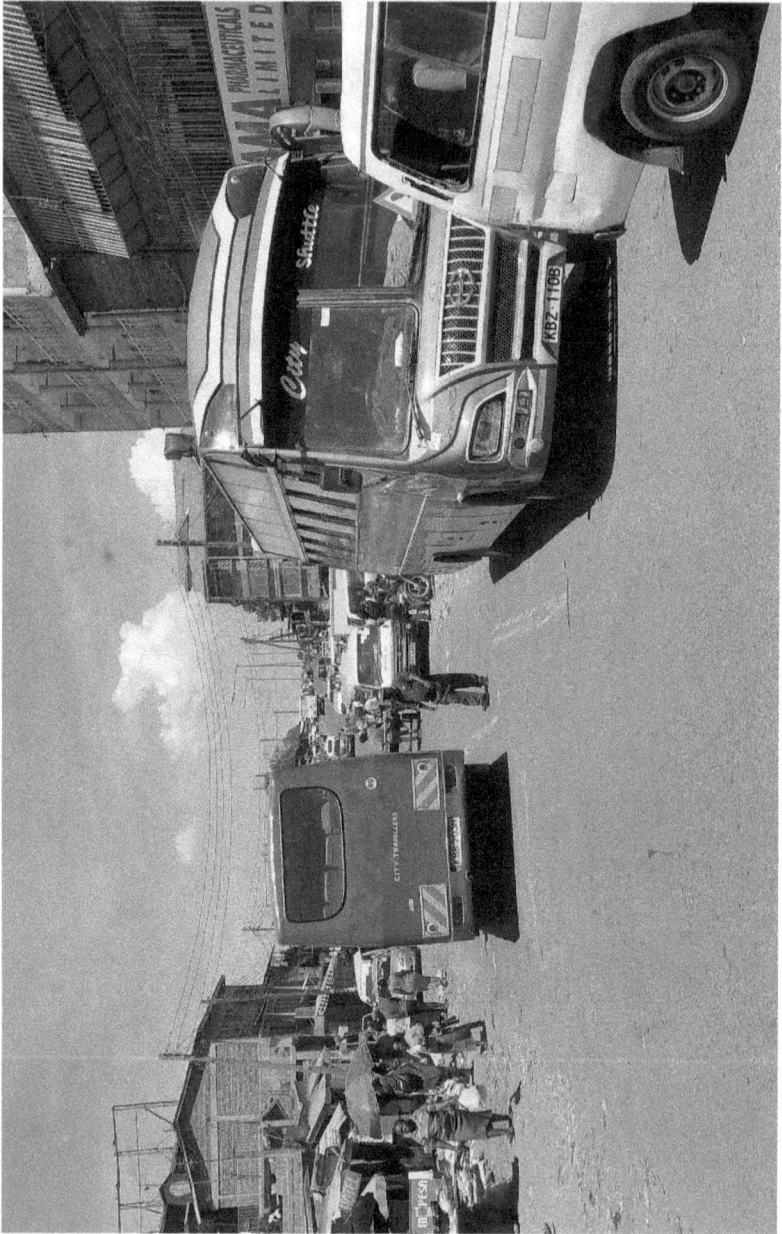

PLATE 7 *Traders, vehicles and pedestrians compete for space in busy areas*

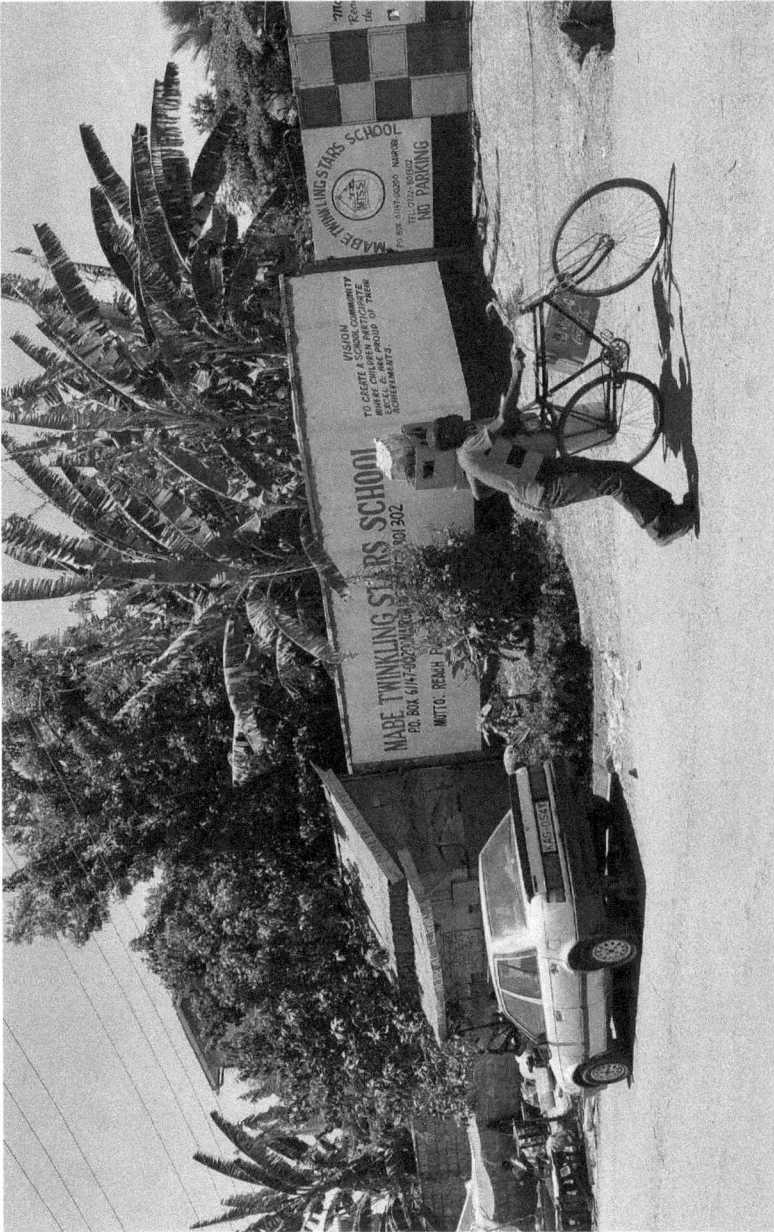

PLATE 8   *Porters play a key role in transporting goods between the producers or wholesalers and the traders in the markets*

PLATE 9   *A clothing market that sells both new and secondhand goods*

PLATE *10 Stalls selling wood, cosmetics, shoes and fresh produce*

PLATE *11 A trader selling wood, sand, bricks and other building materials from his yard*

PLATE *12 Selling sugar cane*

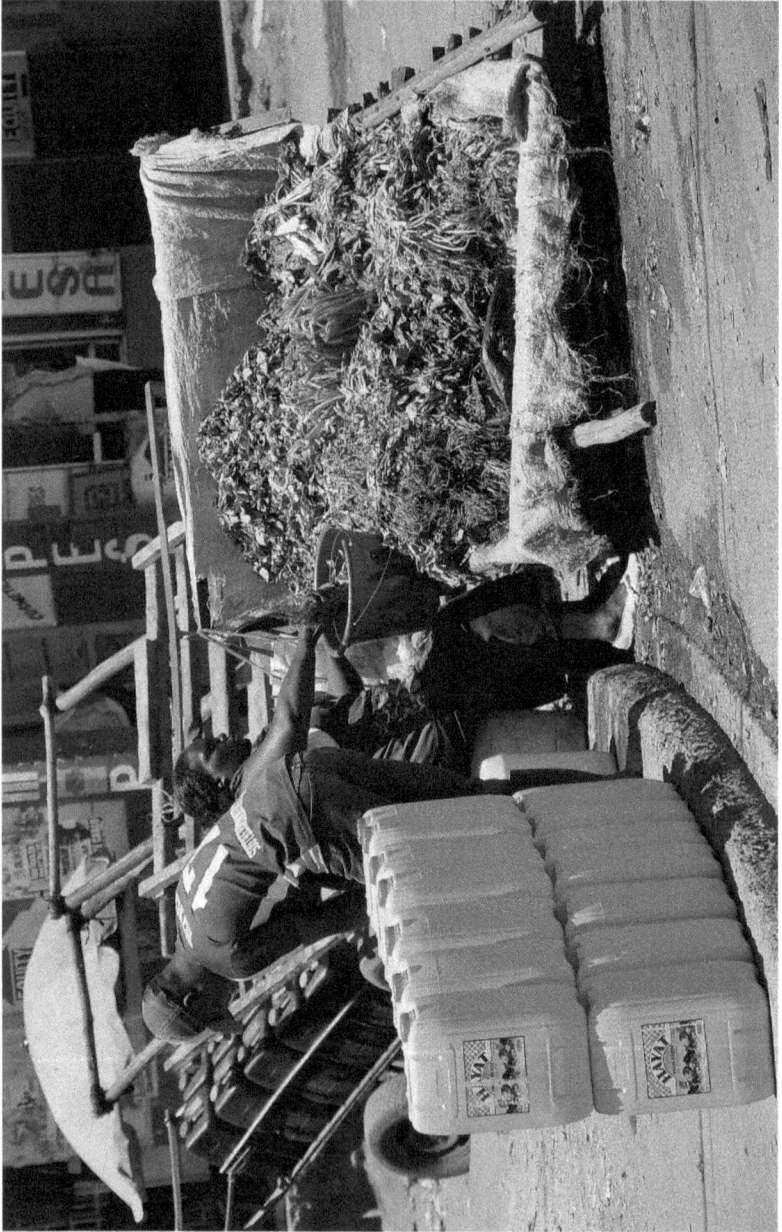

PLATE 13 *Potable water for sale with fresh vegetables*

PLATE *14 Banana sellers outside an allocated market area*

PLATE 15 *Scrap metal, secondhand tools and electrical equipment*

Chapter 9

Towards the formation of autonomous communities

In this chapter, I discuss mechanisms of self- and group regulation within the traders' associations that enable the markets to function as autonomous communities. I show how rules and regulations are formulated and how individuals are mandated to implement these. I outline incentives for compliance and punishments for non-compliance, and provide some insight into how these work.

Good governance is elusive in many African countries at both the state and municipal levels. Patronage and corruption stifle voices of opposition, and political analysts bemoan the relative weakness of democratic institutions on the continent. Disputes often lead to conflict and conflicts lead to wars, leaving states and cities with diminishing resources and little capacity to manage what they have. As Peet (2007: 14) observes, 'the great puzzle is how society manages to produce a safe system that supports common sense when many people commonly experience a horrific everyday world of poverty, hunger and death'.

Given this context, what keeps thousands of market traders and artisans in Nairobi safe and resilient? The fact is that traders and artisans of different genders, ethnic and age groups work reasonably harmoniously together to create and maintain a socio-economic order that enables them to live and thrive economically in communities that are largely autonomous and independent of state support. They, create their own discourse, social imaginaries and institutions to regulate power, ensure good governance and manage class distinctions. In an attempt to offer some insight into how they accomplish all this, I draw on concepts put forward by Michel Foucault (1969) on the construction of discourse, Douglass North (1990) on regulatory mechanisms, and Richard Peet (2007) on power sharing, and apply these to what I observed in markets in Nairobi.

According to Foucault, discourse facilitates social order. Discourse consists of the viewpoints and positions from which people speak and act. Given that government think-tanks, city officials and banking associations are largely absent from Nairobi's marketplaces, their discourse is directed by market veterans. These are individuals who have invited many artisans and traders into the markets and therefore enjoy loyalty and support. They often have special skills and charisma and symbolise success. Narratives developed around them drive and shape a discourse that legitimises the work of earning a living in a market. The veterans themselves also often narrate the stories of individuals and households that have secured their freedom from poverty and are successfully meeting their basic needs for food and shelter, and are able to care for and educate their children.

For example, the axioms *wira ni wira* (any type of work is still work) and *kazi ni kazi, bora unga* (any type of work is still work as long as it enables one to buy maize meal) are often used to validate work outside of the formal sector. These truisms justify and rationalise working in a market and encourage individuals not to feel inferior to those who have formal jobs in the city. Similarly, the song *Waigwa ngihuha Kihuni thenga thengera* (If you hear me whistling, give way) acknowledges the role of porters who carry goods on their backs between the markets and bus stops and whistle to alert fellow pedestrians that they are carrying a heavy load.

Popular discourse linked to artisans and traders projects markets as spaces in which the drama of human resilience is enacted, and where willpower, endurance, courage and the desire for life and nurturing are ever present. The resilience they show in running the markets is expressed in the song *Mucibi wa Marigiti* (Market belt) in which a singer narrates the story of how his mother paid for his university degree by working as a trader. As a result, he was able to get an interesting job with a good salary and he showed his appreciation by building her a house. The song helps underline the idea that those who are willing to share the little they have for the good of others will achieve their goals and their generosity will be reciprocated.

The socio-economic imaginary

The primary discourse of older traders is geared towards constructing a socio-economic imaginary related to improving families' quality of life and households' built environments. Their vision is about identifying possibilities in difficult situations and enhancing a consciousness that hardships don't last forever. To avoid self-blame and demoralisation when times are tough, success and failure are attributed to divine intervention. As one trader put it, 'It is God who has blessed a fellow trader, therefore my turn will come.' This view probably helps to reduce interpersonal conflicts that might otherwise be generated by petty jealousies and it enhances the sense of solidarity between traders and artisans.

Traders and artisans know how marginalised they are. They are fully aware that the national and local governments are against them and do little to prioritise their interests. When the government launches infrastructure maintenance and improvement programmes, the marketplaces are usually excluded. Roads, pathways, buildings and toilet facilities in traders' and artisans' spaces are never repaved or renovated. While street cleaners are a common sight in the centre of the city and in the higher-income suburbs, city council staff are seldom seen cleaning in or near the market precincts. Of course, traders feel ignored and exploited because they pay rates but receive so few services. Nevertheless, they choose not to be preoccupied with matters beyond their control. They are aware that such preoccupations stifle the spirit and make one's own efforts and relationships less meaningful. Instead, therefore, they choose to concentrate on the work at hand and build on what they have rather than bemoan what they lack.

Occasionally, they do act together to express their anger at city officials through protests and demonstrations. For example, in 2015, after a fire at City Park Market on Limuru Road, traders stoned Nairobi's governor, Evans Kidero, when he arrived to address them.[62] In 2012, a similar level of anger was demonstrated when Gikomba traders and artisans demonstrated against import duties outside police headquarters. These kinds of social protests and demonstrations are not an everyday occurrence in Nairobi. They occur when traders and artisans feel their livelihoods are seriously threatened by external factors. They generally prefer not to engage in actions that interfere with their work or affect their own social order.

Their belief in a higher being also helps the traders and artisans to imagine a future when conditions will be less grim even though grim conditions tend to be the order of the day for many – customers are few, costs increase, creditors default and city authorities repeatedly serve eviction notices. The weather is often a factor making the markets too hot, rainy or muddy. Outbreaks of fire are a constant threat. Attributing causality to a higher being assuages traders' pain and uncertainty and helps them imagine better times.

Structures for dialogue and conflict resolution

Creating a peaceful working environment is a key feature of the traders' and artisans' socio-economic imaginary. Their attitude can be summed up in the phrase 'bear up and let go'. To facilitate this, they have created associations that enhance dialogue and peer arbitration so that everyday problems can be resolved quickly and pragmatically. Led by elected representatives and overseen by boards of trustees, these associations are geared towards preventing, reducing and ending any conflicts that might affect the ability of traders to focus on securing their own livelihoods.

Solidarity and connectedness are crucial aspects of how the associations function, as was demonstrated when all the traders at Uhuru Market closed their businesses after a fire gutted the market's D Block; they also worked together to fundraise for the building of a new block. Similarly, traders and artisans from across many different markets attended the funeral of the chairperson of the Kamukunji Jua Kali Association when he died in 2014.

Human beings, as North (1990) observes, realise social order by creating institutions that regulate our behaviour. Artisans and traders are no exception. They have rules to regulate day-to-day transactions and general conduct, so upholding the common good and ensuring the basic safety of the traders. The rules address the many issues that can affect the smooth running of the market, and aim to reduce conflict and friction. Pragmatic in nature and negotiated by the parties most affected, the rules define what is expected from artisans and traders in terms of production, exchange, the sharing of space and the handling of customers. Many of the rules have been passed down through generations of traders and artisans but new ones are negotiated and agreed upon as new issues arise; mostly they are unwritten and disseminated orally.

Every trader and artisan is responsible for ensuring that the rules are respected and individuals oversee one another's conduct. The strong ties of family, friendship and ethnicity that link traders to one another within the associations probably enhance their willingness to abide by the rules. However, all market associations have disciplinary committees which also play important roles in coordinating the enforcement of rules and regulations.[63]

As in most business communities, disputes do occur. The most common ones include issues related to pricing, customers, employees, space, theft, debt, rental rates, how to respond to the city council, the management of the market and invasion by uninvited hawkers, which leads to overcrowding. Other more personal issues relate to ethnic and generational divides, and individual conduct related to anything from cleanliness, gossiping, tardiness or drunkenness to defaulting on a loan, failure to contribute or remit money to a social group or committing fraud and embezzlement. The copying of products and designs also causes trouble between artisans.

In general, individual traders first try to address disputes through talking directly to one another. Where this fails to resolve matters, the associations get involved. The offenders present their case to the association's disciplinary committee and then witnesses are called. Elders or respected people in the cluster will often arbitrate. Sometimes, those who initiated a conflict are named and shamed or isolated; sometimes they have to pay a penalty. In extreme cases, they can be restricted from trading for a certain period or even evicted from the market. However, reconciliation between conflicting individuals is strongly encouraged because relationships in the markets are expected to be long term. In a very few cases, disputes are taken to the police.

To sum up, traders try to prevent disputes through agreeing to rules that apply equally to all. If conflicts do occur, peer-to-peer dialogue is followed by arbitration by their own association's disciplinary committee. This can be followed by a further mediation process, or by naming and shaming or eviction. Local authorities or the police are approached as a last resort.

Power sharing and social order

In *Geography of Power* (2007), Richard Peet suggests that power tends to override many aspects of social order. He argues that power sharing is therefore crucial in achieving social order. Nairobi's Kamukunji Jua Kali Market is interesting in this regard as its artisans have established a power-sharing formula based on ethnicity.

Kamukunji is a multi-ethnic collective of metalworking artisans that has members from the Kikuyu, Kamba, Luhya and Luo ethnic groups. To address the issue of leadership, they decided on a strategy of ethnic inclusion. Seats on the leadership committee are shared on the basis of an agreement that ensures that all ethnic groups are included on the committee and that people from different ethnic groups never compete for the same position. So, if it is decided that the committee will be chaired by the Agikuyu, only Agikuyu artisans will stand for the position of chair and all the different ethnic groups in Kamukunji vote for whichever one of the Agikuyu candidates they prefer. Agreement on the distribution of positions is arrived at before the election is held. This ensures that voters are never divided into ethnic voting blocs that support candidates from their own ethnic group only. It also ensures that all committee members enjoy the support of all groups in the collective. This mechanism undoubtedly helps minimise ethnic disputes that might otherwise divide the market. By acknowledging that ethnicity can be divisive, this system ensures that the issue of ethnicity is addressed fairly and openly rather than denied and suppressed or encouraged and supported. On the basis of the same agreement, positions for women and young leaders have also been created. In essence, the Kamukunji Jua Kali collective has developed a bottom-up leadership practice that successfully addresses the issue of ethnicity while also ensuring that women and youth are represented.

Pricing is the other area that traders and artisans manage in a manner that helps them maintain their sense of community and ensures fairness. Product pricing has the potential to affect collaboration and commitment, especially if two or more traders are selling similar goods in one market. In general, traders agree that to maintain community and fairness, pricing can be done by consensus. Under free-market conditions, business owners are free to adjust prices up or down as they see fit. As shown in Table 9, things work a little differently in Nairobi's markets.

TABLE 9 *Pricing behaviours among traders and artisans in Nairobi, 2015*

Pricing behaviours	Traders		Artisans	
	n	%	*n*	%
Adjust prices freely	148	38.5	113	39.6
Adjust upwards for certain customers	145	37.7	127	44.3
Never adjust upwards	239	62.2	160	55.7
Adjust downwards for certain customers	154	40.1	125	43.7
Never adjust downwards	230	59.9	161	56.3
Increase prices at certain times of the day	98	25.5	55	19.2
Decrease prices at certain times of the day	103	26.8	53	18.9
Keep prices stable all day	286	74.5	232	80.8

These statistics reflect price adjustments made by traders and artisans on the basis of customers and times of the day in different marketplaces. In general, the majority seem to make choices that avoid causing conflict. Most of those spoken to said they wanted to be fair to other traders and artisans by not undercutting them.

Where the pricing of products is complex and likely to cause disharmony, innovative solutions are found. For example, traders in secondhand clothing in Gikomba Market use a system known as Camera. Camera is a form of blind bidding where a bidder is asked to bid for a particular item in a bale before it is opened. The bales contain goods imported by wholesalers from the US and Europe and are sold to traders unopened. That is, bidders offer different amounts for items in the bale without knowing their quality or sizes. The person who bids the highest gets first option when the bale is opened and is followed by the others in order of the sizes of their bids. Camera products always have a higher value and consist of trendy fashion items that are either expensive or difficult to find in local shops. Sometimes, shop owners come and buy these items from the market for resale in city boutiques.

Once all of the best-quality goods in a bale have been bid for, the remaining items are sold through another system known as *kufagia* (literally. sweeping). In this process, every item is available for the same price, enabling traders to sell the remaining goods at a price that ensures they at least break even. The process involves applying the following formula: the bale buying price plus the intended profit per bale minus the cash in hand (based on all that has been sold from the bale through the Camera process). The amount derived from this calculation is divided by the number of items left in the bale to get the *kufagia* price for each item. The traders then negotiate for a price based on the number of items on offer and their quality. Once they agree on this, the deal is sealed. If they cannot agree, the seller is likely to continue selling the bale on an item by item basis. If they do agree, *kufagia* items are sold into lower-income neighbourhoods in both rural and urban areas. This enables the traders to buy a large volume of goods at an affordable price and reduces the hassle of going to select items from various bale openers.

Chapter 10

Cultural villages: Broadening the model

In developing the analytical framework used in this book, I explored several perspectives on the cultural evolution of cities. In Europe and North America, research highlighting the central role of culture in urban regeneration is becoming increasingly important (see, for example, Santatagata 2002; Stern and Seifert 2010). In those contexts, the term 'cultural district' is used to describe territorial complexes that cluster around certain characteristic features. These can vary widely, encompassing features as divergent as technology, finance, law, culture and history. Cultural districts can be defined as agglomerations of local economies in which residents and businesses have a tradition of collaborating with each other for survival and growth. This banding together creates a basis for synergy that stimulates regional growth that is often supported by strong creative and cultural practices linked to music, theatre, galleries and museums. People live, work and spend their leisure time in these cultural districts, and they are seen as holding great potential help to revitalise inner-city areas.

In a similar way, I use the term 'cultural village' to encapsulate the potential of the utu-ubuntu business model to impact positively on the emergent African metropolis. I use the concept as an analytical category that includes the transactional and cultural practices of traders and artisans, as well as those who benefit from the markets they establish. What I am suggesting is that the cultural and business practices that make traditional African markets into effective and vibrant urban growth points deserve both recognition and further research within the field of global urban practice. In this chapter, I suggest possible strategies for blending African logic, norms and values into global urban theory on cultural districts, and I outline how urban planners and policy-makers can use the notion of cultural villages to enhance inclusivity and sustainability in urban planning. The concept of the cultural village offers a useful frame through which the institutional meanings, logics, strategies, norms and values of traders and artisans can be viewed as they make a living and imprint themselves on the city. This frame also ensures that those who live and work on (what are typically seen as) the margins of urban space are acknowledged as intentional agents who are aware of their inextricable links with one another and who are negotiating their livelihoods both as individuals *and* as part of a community.

Planning for inclusivity

Khayesi, Monheim and Nebe (2010) have done important work on outlining the potentials that lie in transport policies and practices that aim to create 'streets for all' – catering for pedestrians, cyclists, street vendors and so on, as well as public and private motor vehicles. In my view, this vision needs to be extended to urban planning as a whole, based on the realisation that people come to the city with different worldviews. Of course, city authorities have to try to balance these worldviews and ensure social justice in terms of how socio-economic organisation manifests spatially. However, for one worldview to dominate planning, as the Western model currently does, at the expense of others, is simply wrong. The informal sector, which largely reflects the mindset of the majority of Nairobi's citizens, must be brought back into city planning.

The construction of residential settlements without considering where their inhabitants will work, worship, park, shop or spend their leisure time is common in African cities. Despite this, as shown in Plates 7–15, traders and artisans make inroads in these spaces, squeezing their stalls between buildings and occupying any free space they can find. They do this in an attempt to sustain their own livelihoods as well as supply goods and services to residents of these areas. This occurs as a result of the short-sightedness of the architects, planners and property developers who have failed over and over again to cater for the needs of residents, as well as for the traders and artisans who step in to supply them with necessary goods and services. Too many urban planners and developers seem to be utterly unaware of the need for such businesses, and even more so of the values and norms according to which these businesses operate and which should be considered in planning.

Why is it necessary to point out to planners that people in poorer residential areas also need access to food, utensils, toiletries, snacks and clothes (sometimes in very small quantities, depending on their disposable incomes)? Surely it is time for planners, architects and property developers to think creatively about how and where traders and artisans can be accommodated and included. The fact that this is still not happening indicates the urgent need for dialogue between traders, artisans, policy-makers, planners and investors about urban planning and infrastructure development.

City planners must recognise that traders, artisans and peasants are as human as the middle class. They deserve to be accommodated in the built environment like anyone else. For example, at Dagoretti Corner, a cluster of furniture makers occupy the right side of the verge. On the left verge are plant sellers. Together, they create congestion and delay both vehicles and pedestrians. This is typical of many areas in Nairobi. To create a built environment that is efficient, safe and comfortable for traders, artisans and peasants, as well as for pedestrians and shoppers, schoolchildren and factory workers, planners and property developers need to start co-conceptualising the built environment with *all* of its users and inhabitants.

Open and ongoing dialogue between all these groups has the potential to ensure the creation of spaces and buildings that respond to everyone's needs as opposed to excluding the needs of the poorer members of the community, thereby forcing them into peripheral spaces such as the roadsides at key intersections. Admittedly, some property developers are attempting to accommodate traders and artisans on the ground floors of their buildings but this is not systematic and it is not happening enough.

Learning from the utu-ubuntu model

If Tutu (1999) is correct that the philosophy of utu-ubuntu has the potential to serve as Africa's contribution to global sustainable development, city planners and administrators should look to this for *practical strategies* related to inclusive and sustainable development. As shown in previous chapters, the utu-ubuntu model invites and accommodates the sharing of space and resources in ways that facilitate individual and business resilience.

Because the utu-ubuntu business model involves sharing, generosity, community, accommodation and inclusiveness, its propagation could help reduce greed and cut-throat competition as well as the inequalities that this creates. Were it to cross-fertilise into global business culture, the utu-ubuntu model could transform the nature of urbanisation, prioritising the values of shared humanity, solidarity and compassion. By advocating a sharing of space and resources, and prioritising community relations and conviviality, the model undermines the modernist worldview of the survival of the fittest, thereby potentially reducing conflict over scarce resources.

Traders and artisans can also offer practical lessons on how self-regulating autonomous communities can work. Given the polarisation and sectarianism evident in contemporary cities and states, we have much to learn from the traders' and artisans' practical skills in community building. The Kamukunji electoral process and the Camera system used in Gikomba described in earlier chapters are examples of processes that include all stakeholders, balance individual and group interests and reduce the potential for conflict based on ethnic identity. These strategies for negotiating leadership positions in diverse communities, and for working in ways that facilitate fair exchange, help to keep community relations harmonious and ensure that no single group dominates at the expense of others.

Collaborative planning arises from a recognition of the fact that everyone has a right to the city. The cultural village concept builds on this by recognising that everyone belongs to a community. Inclusive cities require rule setting that regulates individuals and groups while also harmonising their different interests. For example, if Nairobi were to adopt this approach, traders' and artisans' associations would be represented on management committees and stakeholder bodies citywide. Rather than allowing two economic systems to operate in parallel, the city authorities would endeavour to learn about traders' and artisans' models of communality and to understand what it means for a business to be embedded in the realms of the individual, the community and the divine. Similarly, traders and artisans would need to be more open to incorporation into the city's administrative systems. Both sides would have to accept that they cannot always have things their way.

So far, traders and artisans have actively built up some of the self-developed spaces such as Mwiki, Githurai and Kahawa Jua Kali, and must acknowledge that they need support and expert advice in relation to property development. However, outside experts will have to try to understand the traders' value systems and respect the limitations they set. In the past, traders and artisans have been expected to 'catch up' and conform with urban planning models that suit the needs of the elite and middle classes in so-called world-class cities. Instead, Kenya's planners, architects and financiers should try to develop plans and sites based on traders' and artisans' needs, aesthetics and resources, acknowledging, for example, that traders and artisans tend to fear debt and prefer to build in phases as they accumulate the necessary savings. Workable standards and innovative inclusive and enabling practices will be required.

Creating a sense of belonging

What I am calling cultural villages would be agglomerations of local economic and community practices, and would include providers of educational and health services. I call these villages, rather than districts, because they are based on the logic of a group of people who obtain land on which they build their own houses and some of their own infrastructure. Property rights would range from no titles (for land in slums)[64] to individual property rights in the self-developed urban fringes and family or individual rights in the urbanised villages. Residents of these villages would undertake to respect, 're-member' and restore African traditions rather than, as tends to be the case in the cultural districts of Europe and North America, waiting for city authorities or private developers to initiate development.

The process of creating the cultural villages would have to be led by individuals, social or family groups. Their economic base would derive from activities spearheaded by local traders and artisans. Space would be allocated for cultural and leisure activities, including reading, art and worship. School and literacy programmes would be designed to advance cultural knowledge and to equip residents to find technical or social solutions to any problems that arise in the community. Village schools would also bind communities by providing lifelong education. Clinics and community programmes would cater for the community's well-being.

This cultural village concept has the potential to create a sense of belonging among residents as well as giving individuals and communities a sense of identity. If they feel they belong, residents are far more likely to deploy their resources and energies on social and civic activities that might benefit the village. These activities might be anything from keeping areas clean and beautiful to supporting each other in times of stress.

Cultural villages differ from the upgrading programmes that city authorities tend to implement in slums and other low-income settlements in that they can be driven by associations of plot owners, residents, traders, or by property investors and others. They should not be imposed on communities as if they are helpless or superfluous but rather driven by communities that want to participate in improving their neighbourhoods.

Three Gikuyu proverbs are apposite here: *thina nduri miri* (poverty has no roots and is not permanent), *kamuingi koyaga ndiri* (a group can lift a heavy pestle, i.e. unity is strength) and *gweterera ti kuinaina* (patience is not cowardice). They express the importance

164

of continuing to hope for change, and of showing solidarity and patience in difficult circumstances, be they personal or shared. They illustrate the principle behind cultural villages – that anyone can lift themselves out of poverty if they act in solidarity with others. And they suggest that even if cultural villages take time to evolve, they will eventually take shape and the waiting will be worthwhile. Patience is particularly relevant to the process of funding the necessary infrastructural projects. However, if established using the principles of utu-ubuntu, family, neighbourhood or social groups are likely to develop innovative social and self-financing mechanisms such as those used by the traders and artisans described in this book.

Imprinting African logic, norms and values

In colonial times, Christians and other Westerners denounced African education, art, clothing, cuisine, dance and culture, declaring it devilish and primitive. Africans who aspired to join the surge towards modernity were encouraged to discard and deny their culture and heritage. A reclaiming and deepening of this culture could take place through the establishment of small private family- and community-based museums, theatres and community halls. Undoubtedly, the restoring, curating and preserving of what existed before would deepen communities sense of their own worth; it could also help to document the process of transformation and resistance expressed in the persistence of the utu-ubuntu philosophy.

Towns and cities with long-held traditions related to architecture, the arts, food and sport are favourite tourist destinations worldwide. Similarly, every community should be encouraged to bring their own creative energies and unique cultural practices into the African metropolis. Individuals moving into Nairobi's self-developed urban fringes and urbanised villages should be encouraged to bring their diverse cultural experiences with them, thereby shaping the built environment and enriching the city's culture. Equally, cultural villages could provide space for communities to narrate their histories and address the critical issues that will help them map out their futures. Essentially, communities should help to confer identities on their cities and vice versa. Cultural villages could help to foster and expand utu-ubuntu-based relations not only between traders and artisans but between all residents of the city.

The further development of cultural villages would involve designing spaces and built environments that are illuminated by sharing, collaboration, inclusivity and community. Policy-makers, planners and investors could enhance the sustainability of African cities by helping to transform them into a collection of cultural villages in which people can live, work and advance their culture. Land-use models could be informed by existing imaginaries of built environments. These include thatched roofs, communal workshops, communal orchards and vegetable beds, and shared animal and poultry sheds. This would not only provide living and working spaces that enhance food security but also help to preserve traditional farming practices and add green spaces to the city. To include such imaginaries in urban planning, architects, planners and city managers will need to work with residents to agree on regulations regarding cleanliness, noise, pollution and the general look of the built environment. It will also involve determining the optimal size for such areas and zoning parts of the city accordingly.

Cultural villages could also document and curate their own transformation. This would include noting changes in house shapes and sizes, building materials, lighting, energy, water resources, furniture, cooking technologies and eating utensils. The evolution of infrastructure and means of transport from walking paths to cycle paths to roads could also be documented. Other interesting shifts worth documenting include attitudes to, and use of, indigenous vegetables as well as systems of measures and weights used in markets.

Entrenching local economies

Another goal of developing cultural villages is to strengthen local economies. Creative activities that involve production and exchange invariably attract tourists and other local citizens who have leisure time and surplus income to spend. At the same time, the creation of cultural villages deepens communities' social and cultural capital as they participate in the exchange, production and consumption of knowledge and technology. Table 10 provides an indication of the kinds of economic activities envisaged.

TABLE 10 Possible activities and products of African cultural villages

Activity	Process	Actors	Products
Museums and archives	Storage, preservation and curation of African cultural practices and artefacts	Individuals, families or social and professional groups	Art, musical instruments, tools, clothing, cuisine, performance, photographs, letters, newsletters, other documents
Theatres, choirs and cultural groups	Performances, workshops for performers, scriptwriters, composers, etc.	Individuals, families, clubs, schools, foundations	Plays, films, books, musical events
Craft and processing workshops	Designing, cutting, dyeing, sewing, welding, firing, repurposing fermenting, brewing, cooking, recycling,	Artisans and traders	Clothing, bags, beadwork, shoes, furniture, skins and hides, woodwork, metalwork, tools, ceramics, milk products, cooked food and preserves
Trading and retailing	Sourcing, stockholding, display and sales	Artisans and traders	Household goods, fresh food and vegetables, garments, shoes, secondhand goods, hardware
Small-scale farming/ kitchen gardening	Composting, sowing, planting, propagating, fertilising, weeding, pruning, harvesting	Farmers, families or co-operatives	Live chickens, goats and cattle, meat products, fruit, vegetables, herbs and spices; enhanced food security

Traditional foods, including *rukuri* (dried meat with honey), *ngarango* (deep fried lard) and *mitura* (roasted intestines), as prepared by the Agikuyu, and *mursik* (sour milk), favoured by the Kalenjin, would feature. Similarly, the fermenting, boiling and roasting of sweet potatoes, arrowroot and yams could replace the snacks sold by multinational companies. Traditional breakfasts and baby foods made from bananas, cassava, sweet potatoes and yams are often popular, as are jams, sauces, dried fruit, and fruit purees made from indigenous fruits.

Artisan craft manufacturers could work with local abattoirs and make use of skins, hides, bones, etc. in the production of garments, shoes, sandals, ornaments, book covers, mats, bags, and so on. In areas where clay is abundant, pottery studios could be developed. Traditional *aturi* (blacksmithing) sites, such as the one near Precious Blood Girls' School in Dagoretti, could be preserved as centres for metalwork and woodwork and also function as a tourist attraction.

Cultural villages lend themselves to the organising of food and harvest festivals, fashion shows, sports events, cultural festivals, and citizen days. Traditional shrines, such as the fig tree in Uthiru, could become valued focal points in a cultural village. Traces of colonial occupation such as Fort Smith, the trading post where the British soldiers were first stationed, could be turned into museums or educational centres.

Art and culture would be enhanced by the revival of traditional dance and the promotion of community theatres similar to the Kamiriithu Community Theatre established by Ngũgĩ wa Thiong'o. Such theatres could narrate and dramatise the everyday struggles and experiences of people as they hustle to earn a living. Some self-developed urban fringes, such as Kahawa Sukari on the outskirts of Nairobi, are already being used as film sets for dramas featured on Kenya's Citizen TV channel, namely *Mother in Law* and *Machachari*. *Mother in Law* shows the intergenerational struggle of a family to maintain solidarity and identity in the context of modernity and diversity. *Machachari* demonstrates community bonding as various characters try to climb the socio-economic ladder.

The urbanised villages of Dagoretti are the setting for another Citizen TV drama, *Papa Shirandula*, which recounts the lives of security guards, gardeners, secretaries, messengers and landladies as they struggle to maintain their sense of identity while modernity makes inroads into their workplaces and homes. Similarly, Kenya Television Network is trying to bring the experiences of life in Kawangware to the fore through its show, *House Helps of Kawangware*. Traders and artisans could join these creative industries as set designers, beauticians, writers, photographers, studio crew, garment makers and set builders.

At a slightly different level, the changing nature of leisure activities should also be curated and documented so that communities can reflect on their experiences. For example, the commodification of meat as seen in the shift from the slaughtering of animals at home to the purchasing of meat in shops and the selling of traditional *nyama choma* (roast meat) by city hotels and restaurants is worthy of study. Similarly, the shift from household brewing and drinking, with the use of *ruhia* (horns) and *mbakuri* (bowls), to the rise of bars and pubs is worth unpacking. This move has largely excluded women from a key aspect of household recreation and leisure. Women's responses to this, and the overall impact on family life, have been considerable.

The professionalisation of training and mentoring

In line with the search for sustainability, the learning and training that takes place in the African markets could also usefully be linked to curriculums at school and at tertiary level. The traders' and artisans' associations could also help to develop standards for the certification and registration of skills. Schools of fashion design or engineering, for example, could then send students to complete internships at the markets where they could gain some practical experience in the design, manufacturing and selling of goods. Metalworking artisans could train mechanical engineering students in the application of structural designs, while engineering students could reciprocate by training artisans in the use of digitised technologies and operating systems. Where relevant, designs, structures and processes could be documented and even patented in partnership with the universities.

Similarly, Kenya's National Youth Service could be linked to traders' and artisans' learning and mentoring programmes, with the state paying for access to traders' skills and crafts. This would benefit both the state and the traders while nurturing a sense of partnership between them. Traders and artisans could offer their practical and hard-earned experience in trading and crafting while schools and the National Youth Service could back this up with training in aspects such as costing and the use of digital technologies. These kinds of collaborations would further entrench the inclusion and legitimacy of traders and artisans in the urban and national economy.

To sum up, the development of cultural villages will require the participation of a range of experts including planners, architects, surveyors, builders, economists and lawyers. Land owners' associations, residents' associations, tenants' associations, as well as property investors, traders, artisans and peasants will all have to be involved. Ideally, experts should make suggestions on technical matters such as street layout and building quality and should strive to enhance the involvement of traders and artisans when it comes to the use of local resources and adopting the culture of utu-ubuntu in relation to the sharing of designs, technology, innovations, managerial skills and knowledge.

Cultural villages could be financed by individuals, families, social groups and cooperatives that choose to pool their resources for the benefit of their group. This includes accumulating savings over time and making specific investments in communal infrastructure, such as securing water resources, paving roads or adding street lights. Already, such groups have drilled boreholes in Kinoo and provided security in Kahawa Sukari. Individual, family and group funds can be supported by foundations and low-interest loans to avoid long-term indebtedness. In these ways, cultural villages offer great potential to be self-financing and form a solid base for economic activity while affirming cultural identity, documenting community history and creatively building solidarity in terms of governance and inclusivity.

In essence, my findings show that traders and artisans have played, and continue to play, a key role in concentrating labour and capital in Nairobi's marketplaces. In both the colonial and postcolonial states, traders and artisans positioned themselves to resist the capture and colonisation of their spheres of influence using models and traditions handed on to them from previous generations. The weak infrastructure and poor surroundings in which they live do not make them live lesser lives. Like everyone else, they have aspirations and make plans to achieve their goals. With very few resources, they harness their own creativity to devise social innovations that help them face the spatial and personal challenges that every human being faces every day.

The challenge for Kenya, as for many African countries, is to embrace an economic system that reflects the knowledge, needs and economic ethics and experiences of a large majority of citizens. In line with classical urban theory, I have argued that African markets are an agglomeration of labour and capital and should therefore be integral to urban planning and national policy-making. The utu-ubuntu model offers urban planners and policy-makers a framework for urbanisation processes that respect and promote indigenous values of inclusivity and dignity.

In conclusion, I can only echo the hope expressed in my introductory chapter that the light shed here on the ethics and values that underpin the work of traders and artisans in Nairobi, as well as their resilience and positive impact on urbanisation, will inform future discourse on urban economics and planning in African cities. The persistence of indigenous African markets into the 21st century in the context of the hostile or neglectful business and policy environment that they encounter every day makes them worthy of further analysis. An investigation of Afrocentric business ethics is long overdue. Attempting to understand the actions and efforts of traders and artisans *from their own points of view*, and analysing how they organise and get by, might allow for viable methods to be identified of enhancing their integration into global urban models and cultures.

Notes

1 In Kenya, the national examinations system has created a means of social segregation. In other words, individuals' examination results tend to determine which side of the international division of labour they will fall into: the global economy (as represented by multinational firms, international agencies and domestic firms) or the indigenous African economy, which is strongly linked to the rural subsistence economy and the urban subaltern classes.

2 A literal translation of *mbara* is 'war' and *mukimo* is a dish that is cooked on special occasions made from potatoes and pumpkin leaves.

3 District Commissioner to the Town Clerk, 9 October 1936. Hawkers Licence RN/1/59. Kenya National Archives.

4 Mr SM Fichat to District Commissioner, 1942. Hawkers Licence RN/1/59. Kenya National Archives.

5 Tea vendors to the Town Clerk, c.1935. Kenya National Archives.

6 Mr W Evans to the Town Clerk, 13 February 1936. Hawkers' Licence 1935–36 RN/1/59. Kenya National Archives.

7 Indian Christian Union to the Town Clerk, 19 December 1935. Hawkers' Licence 1935–36 RN/1/59. Kenya National Archives.

8 *Sunday Post*, 24 April 1942. Kenya National Archives.

9 Nowadays, traders and artisans buy products from white and Indian business operators but rarely enter into partnerships or trust-based transactions with them for fear of being cheated. In general, white- and Indian-owned businesses are located in distinct parts of the city and enjoy higher status in terms of policy planning, legal status, access to technology and market reach.

10 Interestingly, Nairobi's two oldest marketplaces, Burma and Kariokor, were constructed by the colonial authorities to provide employment for African soldiers who fought in the Second World War.

11 Nairobi City Council, Hawkers Bylaws, 1962. JA/15/5. Kenya National Archives.

12 Council to build 12 schools by 1971, *Daily Nation*, 25 November 1965.

13   K£1 was equivalent to KSh20, but the use of pounds has since been abandoned.
14   Report on Proposed Construction of Hawkers' Kiosks in Nairobi: Phase 1,
     JA/15/5 1976. Kenya National Archives.
15   Council to build 12 schools by 1971, *Daily Nation*, 25 November 1965. Kenya
     National Archives.
16   Kariokor Estate opened: President outlines housing drive, *Daily Nation*,
     19 January 1966. The Commonwealth Development Corporation (CDC) and
     the United States Agency for International Development (USAID) helped fund
     the development of Kariokor Estate to the tune of K£260 000.
17   New Uhuru Estate will ease crisis, *Daily Nation*, 3 August 1967.
18   Mayor opens show house, *Daily Nation* (no date).
19   Keep your houses smart, mayor, *Daily Nation*, 21 November 1969.
20   Police proposal angers Mayor, *Daily Nation*, 5 October 1967.
21   Rubia sees soapy, *Daily Nation*, 19 March 1963.
22   City council to advertise market stalls, *Daily Nation*, 19 December 1966.
23   Market's new look, *Daily Nation*, 4 October 1967.
24   See, for example, Traders ignored quit notice, *Daily Nation*, 2 July 1968.
25   City Council of Nairobi: Conferences and Congresses, 1973 RN/2/1/3. Kenya
     National Archives.
26   Speech of Town Clerk to Conference in Manila, 1973. RN/17/8/14. Kenya
     National Archives.
27   Speech of Town Clerk to Conference in Manila, 1973. RN/17/8/14. Kenya
     National Archives.
28   Speech of Town Clerk to Conference in Manila, 1973. RN/17/8/14. Kenya
     National Archives.
29   City Council of Nairobi: Conferences and Congresses, 1973. RN/2/1/3. Kenya
     National Archives.
30   City commission has outstayed its welcome, *Daily Nation*, 12 March 1989.
31   Mungai criticizes Gumo over kiosks, *Daily Nation*, 31 March 1990.
32   Muoroto commission boss parades askaris, *Daily Nation*, 13 June 1990 (note that
     in East Africa, the word 'askari' refers to a soldier or police officer).
33   W Muya, One step forward, *Daily Nation*, 4 August 1993.
34   World Vision, for example, reportedly participated in educating communities on
     garbage management; see A Diang'a, A cleaner town for city residents,
     Daily Nation, 5 May 1994.
35   J Waimiru, A tale of homelessness, hunger, extreme poverty, *Daily Nation*,
     27 July 1993.
36   Appeal to end graft, *Daily Nation*, 27 July 1997.
37   A Diang'a, A cleaner town for city residents, *Daily Nation*, 5 May 1993.
38   J Ombuor, Drowning in filth, *Daily Nation*, 10 January 1996.
39   M Mathiu, Nairobi in the throes of decay, *Sunday Nation*, 8 June 1997.
40   See G Mathenge, Reclaiming Nairobi from decades of shameful rot,
     Daily Nation, 2 April 2006.
41   City-wide convention on safer Nairobi, *Daily Nation*, 7 November 2004.
42   Putting a new shine on the city, *Daily Nation*, 30 September 2005.

43 Du Bois also called for business to be ethical and conducted for the purposes of social welfare and satisfying human needs and desires rather than for the sole purpose of accumulating wealth. He wrote: 'Let us with one accord, attack the bottom lie that supports graft and greed and selfishness and race prejudice: namely that any decent man [sic] has at any time any right to adopt any calling or profession for the sole end of personal gain' (Du Bois 1987: 1136–1137).

44 Van den Heuwel explains that, in the late 1980s, as the apartheid state in South Africa began to experience serious economic crisis, certain business leaders worked with the liberation movement to establish the Consultative Business Movement. Its aim was to encourage white business owners to support the transfer of political and economic power into the hands of the previously disenfranchised majority. As part of this initiative, the University of the Witwatersrand's School of Business established the South African Management Project, and it was within this project that the African management movement emerged.

45 Quoted in: The rise of Africapitalism, *The Economist,* 13 November 2014.

46 The name of the Agikuyu community in Kenya can be spelled in different ways, including Kikuyu.

47 The word 'estate' in Nairobi is used to refer to suburbs or neighbourhoods.

48 Make Nairobi truly African, *Daily Nation,* 8 January 1964.

49 From a report by the Town Clerk on The Proposed Construction of Hawkers' Kiosks in Nairobi, 1976. Nairobi City Council, JA/15/5. Kenya National Archives.

50 Ibid.

51 Mazrui's book was used as the basis for the documentary series *Africans: Triple Heritage.*

52 S Rule, Kenya Court Rules Tribe not Widow can Bury a Lawyer, *New York Times,* 16 May 1987. https://www.nytimes.com/1987/05/16/world/kenyan-court-rules-tribe-not-widow-can-bury-a-lawyer.html

53 A billion reasons to believe in Africa. https://www.youtube.com/watch?v=xyT_bYUUG6o

54 These are Swahili words for comfort, unity, pulling together and responsibility or power.

55 In response to the arguments by Roy (2015), Simone (2013) and Turok (2014), this evidence of communities naming settlements after their aspirations seems to negate the idea that people in informal settlements feel no sense of permanence about living in cities.

56 The term 'jua kali' means 'hot sun' and is also used to refer to a range of small and micro enterprises in Kenya. The term is used by traders and artisans to refer to themselves and their area-based associations.

57 Slums have grown in this era because fewer and fewer people have permanent jobs. During the rise of neoliberalism in the 1990s, many of Nairobi's lower-paid workers had no option but to move to the slums. Even workers' cooperatives refused to accept members who were on temporary employment contracts. Private sector-led urban development in this period was profit oriented and accessible only to those who already had access to capital, knowledge and

infrastructure. Kenya's economy collapsed and NGOs assumed responsibility for facilitating people's exit from poverty, but to little effect.

58 B Obegi, Meet varsity student who set up hospital to offer free treatment to poor patients, *Standard Digital,* 5 November 2014. https://www.standardmedia.co.ke/lifestyle/article/2000140503/meet-varsity-student-who-set-up-hospital-to-offer-free-treatment-to-poor-patients

59 Resistance to the British occupation was led by Waiyaki wa Hinga, who died while being taken into exile. The road Waiyaki Way is named after him.

60 Unlike utu, the concept of ubuntu has been the subject of more academic and critical study in South Africa (see, for example, Koster 1996; Nussbaum 2003; Sindane and Liebenberg 2000; Tutu 1999).

61 Leaders are elected by the traders and artisans and serve for limited periods on a rotational basis.

62 Kidero booed, heckled and stones pelted at him by angry Nairobians for lazing around, *Kenyan Daily Post,* 9 February 2015.

63 Such associations have also been documented in markets in Lagos where they create bottom-up management practices that are unrelated to state or municipal legislation (Ikioda 2013). As Ikporukpo (2005, quoted in Ikioda 2013) points out, traders in Lagos's fish market resolve conflicts through mediation and without involving the police or other city authorities. According to Ikioda (2013), the associations play an important role in setting guidelines on pricing. This helps to prevent traders from undercutting one another.

64 Admittedly, some slum dwellers build houses that they rent out, thereby claiming some property rights.

References

Achebe C (1959) *Things Fall Apart*. London: Heinemann

African Development Bank (2014) *Tracking Africa's Progress in Figures*. Tunis

Appadurai A (1996) *Modernity at Large: Cultural Dimensions of Globalisation*. Minneapolis: University of Minnesota Press

Appadurai A (2002) Deep democracy: Urban governmentality and the horizon of politics. *Public Culture* 14(1): 21–47

Asquith Commission Report (1945) Report of the Commision on Higher Education in the Colonies, cmd. 6647. London: His Majesty's Stationery Office

Ball P (2004) *Critical Mass*. London: Arrow

Bangura Y (1994) Economic restructuring, coping strategies and social change in Africa. *Development and Change* 25(4): 785–827

Bekker S and Fourchard L (2013) Introduction. In S Bekker and L Fourchard (eds) *Governing Cities in Africa*. Cape Town: HSRC Press

Benediktssen K (2002) *Harvesting Development: The Construction of Fresh Food Markets in Papua New Guinea*. Ann Arbor: University of Michigan Press

Bhengu MJ (2011) *African Economic Humanism: The Rise of an African Economic Philosophy*. Farnham: Gower

Biden J (2011) Remarks by the US vice-president at the Entrepreneurship Summit, Istanbul. https://obamawhitehouse.archives.gov/the-press-office/2011/12/03/remarks-vice-president-joseph-biden-entrepreneurship-summit

Brennan JR (2006) Blood enemies: Exploitation and urban citizenship in the nationalist political thought of Tanzania, 1958–1975. *Journal of African History* 47: 389–413

Bromley R (1978) Introduction: The urban informal sector: Why is it worth discussing? *World Development* 6(9/10): 1033–1039

Burbank JRK (1994) *A Survey of NGOs as Small-Business Development Agencies in Kenya*. Working Paper No. 493, Institute for Development Studies, University of Nairobi

Collier P (2010) The political economy of natural resources. *Social Research* 77(4): 1105–1132

Colony and Protectorate of Kenya (1928) Ordinances 1928. Nairobi

Colony and Protectorate of Kenya (1950) Ordinances 1950. Nairobi

Davis M (2004) *Planet of Slums*. London: Verso

De Dora M (2011, 21 July) Economics should not be divorced from morality. Blogpost on *Rationally Speaking*: an archived blog by Massimo Pigliucci. http://rationallyspeaking.blogspot.co.za/2011/07/economics-should-not-be-divorced-from.html

De Soto H (1989) *The Other Path: The Economic Answer to Terrorism*. New York: Basic

Diamond J (2012) *The World Until Yesterday: What Can We Learn from Traditional Societies?* New York: Viking

Du Bois WEB (1911/1986) The economics of negro emancipation in the United States. *Sociological Review* 4(3): 303–313

Du Bois WEB (1912) The upbuilding of black Durham: The success of the negroes and their value to a tolerant and helpful southern city. *World's Work* 23: 334–338 (Electronic edition made available by the University of North Carolina at Chapel Hill) http://docsouth.unc.edu/nc/dubois/dubois.html

Du Bois WEB (1987) *Writings*. New York: Penguin

Ehinmowo AA and Ibitoye AO (2010) Periodic market: A common marketing feature in Akoko. *Southwest Journal of Geography and Regional Planning* 3(12): 361–364. http://www.academicjournals.org/JGRP

Ernstson H, Lawhon M and Duminy J (2014) Conceptual vectors of African urbanism: 'Engaged theory-making' and 'platforms of engagement.' *Regional Studies* 48(9): 1563–1577. DOI: 10.1080/00343404.2014.892573

Fanon F (1963) *The Wretched of the Earth*. Translated by Richard Philcox. New York: Grove

Ferguson J (2013) Declarations of dependence: Labour, personhood, and welfare in southern Africa. *Journal of the Royal Anthropological Institute* 19: 223–242

Foucault M (1969) *The Archaeology of Knowledge*. London and New York: Routledge.

Frank G (1966) *The Development of Under Development*. Boston: New England Free Press

Gatheru RM (1966) *A Child of Two Worlds*. London: Heinemann

Ghai D (1965) How good is Kenya's plan? *East African Journal* 19–38

Gibson-Graham JK (2006) *Postcapitalist Politics*. Minneapolis: University of Minnesota Press

Giugale M (2014) *Economic Development: What Everyone Needs to Know*. Oxford: Oxford University Press

Gordon Nembhard J (2014) *Collective Courage: A History of African American Cooperative Economic Thought and Practice*. Pennsylvania: Penn State University Press

Grabski J (2012) 'You can find anything at the Marché Colobane.' In *Dakar's Market Imaginary*. A YouTube playlist. https://www.youtube.com/watch?v=11hax3NXWCg

Gudeman S (2001) *The Anthropology of Economy: Community, Market and Culture.* Oxford: Blackwell

Guha R (1999) *Elementary Aspects of Peasant Insurgency in Colonial India.* Durham, NC: Duke University Press

Guyer JI (2015) Markets and urban provisioning: Context and concepts. In C Monga and J Yifu Lin (eds) *The Oxford Handbook of Africa and Economics: Volume 1.* Oxford: Oxford University Press

Hagen EE (1963) How economic growth begins: A theory of social change. *Journal of Social Issues* 19(1): 20–34. DOI: 10.1111/j.1540-4560.1963.tb00428.x

Harris J (2014) The messy reality of agglomeration economies in urban informality: Evidence from Nairobi's handicraft industry. *World Development* 61: 102–113

Hart K (1973) Informal income opportunities and urban employment in Ghana. *Journal of Modern African Studies* 11(1): 61–89

Hart K, Laville J and Cattani AD (2010) *The Human Economy: A Citizen's Guide.* London: Polity

Heintz J (2012) *Informality, Inclusiveness, and Economic Growth: An Overview of Key Issues.* SIG Working Paper 2012/2, IDRC, Ottawa.

Hodder BW (1969) Rural periodic day markets in part of Yoruba land. *Transactions of the Institute of British Geographers* 65(2): 149–151

Holston J (1998) Spaces of insurgent citizenship. In Leonie Sandercock (ed.) *Making the Invisible Visible: A Multicultural Planning History.* Berkeley: University of California Press

Honwana A (2012) *The Time of Youth Work: Social Change and Politics in Africa.* Bloomfield: Kumarian Press

Hoselitz BF (1952) Entrepreneurship and economic growth. *American Journal of Sociology* 12(1) 97–111. DOI: 10.1111/j.1536-7150.1952.tb00480.x

Hydén G (1994) Party, state and civil society: Control versus openness. In JD Barkan (ed.) *Beyond Capitalism Versus Socialism in Kenya and Tanzania.* Boulder: Lynne Rienner

Hydén G (2014) The economy of affection: Important as ever in Tanzania. Paper presented to the Nordic Africa Institute Development Policy Forum, 18 June

Ikioda F (2013) Urban markets in Lagos, Nigeria. *Geography Compass* 7(7): 517–526

Ikporukpo CO (2005) Ethnicity and social networks in a fish-marketing system, Warri, Nigeria. In G Porter and F Lyon (eds) *Investigations on Building a Food Marketing Policy Evidence Base in Nigeria.* http://community.dur.ac.uk/nigerian.marketing/

ILO (2000) *Employment and Social Protection in the Informal Sector.* Geneva

ILO (2002) *Women and Men in the Informal Economy: A Statistical Picture.* Geneva

Iroegbu P (n.d.) On the notion of culture and colonialism as impediment to economic models of development and democracy in Africa: With a comment on didactic Obama-truce-culture approach. *Gamji.* http://www.gamji.com/article8000/NEWS8418.htm

Iyam D (2013) Continuity and change in female fattening ritual in south-eastern Nigeria. Paper presented at the Annual Meeting of the ASA. http://ssrn.com/abstract=2237343

Jazeel T (2014) Subaltern geographies: Geographical knowledge and postcolonial strategy. *Singapore Journal of Tropical Geography* 35(1): 88–103

Jenkins P (2014) *Urbanisation, Urbanism and Urbanity in an African City.* New York: Palgrave

Johnson S (2012) The rift revealed: The search for financial inclusion in Kenya and the missing social dimension. Paper presented at the Institute for Development Studies, University of Nairobi

Kamete AY (2007) Cold-hearted, negligent and spineless? Planning, planners and the (re) ejection of filth in urban Zimbabwe. *International Planning Studies* 12(2): 153–171

Kamete AY (2013) On handling urban informality in southern Africa. *Geografiska Annaler: Series B, Human Geography* 95(1): 17–31

Khayesi M, Monheim, H and Nebe JM (2010) Negotiating 'streets for all' in urban transport planning: The case for pedestrians, cyclists and street vendors in Nairobi, Kenya. *Antipode* 42(1): 103–126

King AD (1990) *Urbanism, Colonialism and the World Economy: Cultural and Spatial Foundations of the World Urban System.* London: Routledge

King K (1996) *Jua Kali Kenya: Change and Development in an Informal Economy, 1970–1995.* London: James Currey

Kinyanjui MN (2007) Emerging production systems in conventional development: Experiences of the jua kali economy in Kenya. *Umoja Bulletin* 2, Journal of the African and African American Studies Program, Grand Valley State University

Kinyanjui MN (2010) *Social Relations and Associations in the Informal Sector in Kenya.* Social Policy and Development Paper 43, United Nations Research Institute for Social Development. http://www.unrisd.org/80256B3C005BCCF9/ (httpAuxPages)/E9CBDC63008BB214C12576DA00589211/$file/Kinyanjui-pp.pdf

Kinyanjui MN (2011) Jua Kali: Strategies for socio-economic change. *Hemispheres* 26: 29–46

Kinyanjui MN (2012) *Vyama Institutions of Hope: Ordinary People's Market Coordination and Society Organization.* Nairobi: Nsemia

Kinyanjui MN (2013) Women informal garment traders in Taveta Road Nairobi: From the margins to the centre. *Africa Studies Review* 56(3): 147–164

Kinyanjui MN (2014) *Women and the Informal Economy in Urban Africa: From the Margins to the Centre.* London: Zed

KNBS (Kenya National Bureau of Statistics) (2014) *Economic Survey.* Nairobi

Koster JD (1996) Managing the Transformation. In K Bekker (ed.) *Citizen Participation in Local Government.* Pretoria: Van Schaik

La Porta R and Shleifer A (2014) Informality and development. *Journal of Economic Perspectives* 28(3): 109–126

Lefebvre H (1974/1991) *The Production of Space.* Translated by Donald Nicholson-Smith. Oxford: Blackwell

Lewis WA (1954) Economic development with unlimited supplies of labour. *The Manchester School* 22(2): 139–191. DOI: 10.1111/j.1467-9957.1954.tb00021.x

Leys C (1975) *Underdevelopment in Kenya: The Political Economy of Neo-Colonialism.* Berkeley: University of California Press

Leys C (1994) African capitalists and development. In BJ Berman and C Leys (eds) *African Capitalists in African Development.* Boulder: Lynne Rienner

Lindell I (2010) The changing politics of economic informality: Collective organizing, alliances and scales of engagement. In I Lindell (ed.) *African Informal Workers: Collective Agency, Alliances and Transnational Organizing.* London: Zed

Lipton M (1982) *Development and Underdevelopment in Historical Perspective.* London: Methuen

Lutz DW (2009) African ubuntu philosophy and global management. *Journal of Business Ethics* 84: 313–328. DOI: 10.1007/s10551-009-0204-z

Lyons M and Brown A (2007) Seen but not heard: Extending urban citizenship to informal street traders. Paper presented at a conference of the Nordic Africa Institute, Uppsala, 20–22 April

Maathai W (2004) Nobel Lecture, Oslo, 10 December. https://www.nobelprize.org/nobel_prizes/peace/laureates/2004/maathai-lecture-text.html

Macharia K (1997) *Social and Political Dynamics of the Informal Economy in African Cities: Nairobi and Harare.* Lanham: University Press of America

Maloney WF (1999) Does informality imply segmentation in urban labour markets? Evidence from sectoral transitions in Mexico. *World Bank Economic Review* 13(2): 275–302

Maloney WF (2004) Informality revisited. *World Development* 32(7): 1159–1178

Masaru N and Badenoch N (2013) Why periodic markets are held: Considering products, people and place in the Yunnan–Vietnam border area. *Southeast Asian Studies* 2(1): 171–192

Mazrui A (1986) *The Africans: A Triple Heritage.* New York: Little Brown

Mbembe JA and Nuttall S (2004) Writing the world from an African metropolis. *Public Culture* 16(3): 347–372

Mbiti JS (1969) *African Religions and Philosophy.* Nairobi: Heinemann

McClelland D (1961) *The Achieving Society.* Princeton: Nostrand

McCormick D (1999) African enterprise clusters and industrialisation: Theory and reality. *World Development* (Special Issue on Enterprise Clusters) 27(9): 1531–1551

McFarlane C (2011) *Learning the City: Knowledge and Translocal Assemblage.* London: Wiley Blackwell

Meagher K (2007) Manufacturing disorder: Liberalization, informal enterprise and economic 'ungovernance' in African small firm clusters. *Development and Change* 38(3): 473–450

Meagher K (2012) Weber meets Godzilla: Social networks and the spirit of capitalism in East Asia and Africa. *Review of African Political Economy* 39(132): 261–278

Miraftab F (2009) Insurgent planning: Situating radical planning in the global south. *Planning Theory* 8(1): 32–50. DOI: 10.1177/1473095208099297

Mitra IK, Samaddar R and Sen S (eds) (2017) *Accumulation in Post-Colonial Capitalism.* Singapore: Springer

Mitullah WV (2003) Street vending in African cities: A synthesis of empirical findings from Kenya, Côte d'Ivoire, Ghana, Zimbabwe, Uganda and South Africa. Background paper prepared for the *World Development Report, 2005*

Mkandawire T (2014) The spread of economic doctrines and policy making in postcolonial Africa. *African Studies Review* 57(1): 171–198

Moser CO (1978) Informal sector or petty commodity production: Dualism or dependence in urban development. *World Development* 6(9/10): 1041–1064

Mullei A and Bokea C (1999) Introduction. In A Mullei and C Bokea (eds) *Micro and Small Enterprises in Kenya: Agenda for Improving the Policy Environment.* Nairobi: International Centre for Economic Growth

Myers G (2011) *African Cities: Alternative Visions of Urban Theory and Practice.* London: Zed

Namusonge GS (1999) Entrepreneurship development. In A Mullei and C Bokea (eds) *Micro and Small Enterprises in Kenya: Agenda for Improving the Policy Environment.* Nairobi: International Centre for Economic Growth

Ndi A (2007) Metropolitanism, capital and patrimony: Theorizing the postcolonial West African city. *African Identities* 5(2): 167–180

Ngugi J (1965) *The River Between.* London: Heinemann

Ngwalla TA (2011) The planning development challenges of micro retail/shops in Luthuli Avenue of the central business district. Unpublished dissertation, Planning Research Project, University of Nairobi

Njau G (1973) Nairobi urban study: Strategy for metropolitan growth. Unpublished rapporteurs report. Nairobi City Council

North D (1990) *Institutions, Institutional Change and Economic Performance.* Cambridge: Cambridge University Press

Nussbaum B (2003) African culture and ubuntu: Reflections of a South African in America. *Nordic Journal of African Studies* 17: 1–12

Nyeko MM (2014) The banana eater. In EW Allfrey (ed.) *Africa 39: New Writing from Africa South of the Sahara.* New York: Bloomsbury

Obama BH (1965) Another critique of Sessional Paper No. 10 of 1965: Problems facing our socialism. *East Africa Journal* 26–33

Obama BH (2015) Remarks by President Obama at the Global Entrepreneurship Summit, Nairobi, 25 July. https://ng.usembassy.gov/remarks-president-obama-global-entrepreneurship-summit-july-25-2015/

Ochieng Odhiambo F (1995) *African Philosophy: An Introduction.* Nairobi: Consolata Institute of Philosophy

Parker S (2004) *Urban Theory and the Urban Experience: Encountering the City.* London: Routledge

Parnell S and Pieterse E (eds) (2014) *Africa's Urban Revolution.* London: Zed

p'Bitek O (1966) *Song of Lawino.* Nairobi: EAPH

Peet R (2007) *Geography of Power: Making Global Economic Policy.* London: Zed

Pieterse E and Simone A (eds) (2013) *Rogue Urbanism: Emergent African Cities.* Johannesburg: Jacana

Polanyi K (1944) *The Great Transformation: The Political and Economic Origins of Our Time.* Boston: Beacon

Portes A, Castells M and Benton L (1989) *The Informal Economy: Studies in Advanced and Less Developed Countries*. Baltimore: Johns Hopkins University Press

Prag E (2010) *Entrepot politics: Political struggles over the Dantokpa Marketplace in Cotonou, Benin*. Working Paper 3, Danish Institute for International Studies, Copenhagen

Republic of Kenya (1965) *African Socialism and its Implications for Planning*. http:// www.knls.ac.ke/images/AFRICAN-SOCIALISM-AND-ITS-APPLICATION-TO-PLANNING-IN-KENYA.pdf

Republic of Kenya (2007) *Kenya Vision 2030: A Globally Competitive and Prosperous Kenya*. Nairobi

Riddell JB (1974) Periodic markets in Sierra Leone. *Annals of the Association of American Geographers* 64(4): 541–548

Robertson C (1993) Traders and urban struggle: Ideology and the creation of a militant female underclass in Nairobi, 1960–1990. *Journal of Women's History* 4(3): 9–42

Robertson C (1997) *Trouble Showed the Way: Women, Men and Trade in the Nairobi Area, 1890–1990*. Bloomington: Indiana University Press

Robinson J (2002) Global and world cities: A view off the map. *International Journal of Urban and Regional Research* 26(3): 531–554

Robinson J (2013) The urban now: Theorizing cities beyond the new. *European Journal of Cultural Studies* 16(5): 1–19

Robinson J and Parnell S (2012) (Re)theorizing cities from the global south: Looking beyond neoliberalism. *Urban Geography* 33(4): 593–617

Rodney W (1972) *How Europe Underdeveloped Africa*. London: Bogle-L'Ouverture

Roy A (2007) Urban informality: Towards an epistemology of planning. *Journal of American Planning Association* 71(2): 147–158

Roy A (2009) Why India cannot plan its cities: Informality, insurgency and the idiom of urbanisation. *Planning Theory* 8(1): 76–87

Roy A (2011) Slum dog cities: Rethinking subaltern urbanism. *International Journal of Urban and Regional Research* 35(2): 223–238

Roy A (2013) Slum-free cities of the Asian century: Postcolonial government and the project of inclusive growth. *Singapore Journal of Tropical Geography* 35(1): 136–150 (Special issue on advancing postcolonial geographies). DOI: 10.1111/ sjtg.12047

Roy A (2015) Who's afraid of postcolonial theory? *International Journal of Urban and Regional Research* 40(1): 200–209

Santatagata W (2002) Cultural districts, property rights and sustainable economic growth. *International Journal of Urban and Regional Planning* 261: 9–23

Sanusi SL (2012) Neither the Washington nor Beijing Consensus: Developmental models to fit African realities and cultures. Paper presented at the Eirenicon Africa Public Lecture Series, Royal School of Medicine, London, England, 27 March. http://www.bis.org/review/r120417d.pdf

Schimdtz H and Nadvi K (1999) Clustering and industrialisation: Introduction. *World Development* 27(9): 1503–1514

Scott AJ (2011) Emerging cities of the third wave. *City: Analysis of Urban Trends, Culture, Theory and Policy Action* 15(3–4): 289–321

Scott AJ and Storper M (1986) *Production, Work, Territory: The Geographical Anatomy of Industrial Capitalism.* London: Harper Collins

Scott AJ and Storper M (2014) The nature of cities: The scope and limits of urban theory. *International Journal of Urban and Regional Research* 39(1): 1–15

Sidaway JD, Woon CY and Jacobs JM (2014) Planetary postcolonialism. *Singapore Journal of Tropical Geography* 35(1): 4–21

Simmel G (1903/2002) The metropolis and mental life. In G Bridge and S Watson (eds) *The Blackwell City Reader.* Oxford: Wiley-Blackwell

Simone A (2001) Straddling the divides: Remaking associational life in informal African city. *International Journal of Urban and Regional Research* 25(1): 102–117. DOI: 10.1111/1468-2427.00300

Simone A (2013) Cities of uncertainty: Jarkarta, the urban majority, and inventive political technologies. *Theory, Culture and Society* 30(7/8): 243–263

Sindane J and Liebenberg I (2000) Reconstruction and the reciprocal other: The philosophy and practice of ubuntu and democracy in African society. *Politeia* 19(3): 31–46

Skinner C (2009) Challenging city imaginaries: Street traders' struggles in Warwick Junction. *Agenda* 23(81): 101–109

Spivak G (1988) Can the subaltern speak? In C Nelson and L Grossberg (eds) *Marxism and the Interpretation of Culture.* Champaign: University of Illinois Press

Spivak G (2005) Scattered speculations on the subaltern and the popular. *Postcolonial Studies* 8(4): 475–486

Standing G (2011) *The Precariat: The New Dangerous Class.* London: Bloomsbury

Steck JF, Didier S, Morange M and Rubin M (2013) Informality, public space and urban governance: An approach through street trading (Abidjan, Cape Town, Johannesburg, Lomé and Nairobi). In S Bekker and L Fourchard (eds) *Governing Cities in Africa.* Cape Town: HSRC Press

Stern MK and Seifert SC (2010) Cultural clusters: The planning implication of cultural assets, agglomeration for neighbourhood revitalization. *Journal of Planning Education and Research* 29: 262–279

Stiglitz J (2015) *Inequality, Wealth, and Growth: Why Capitalism is Failing?* (Video) http://www.mediatheque.lindau-nobel.org/videos/33963/joseph-stiglitz/laureate-stiglitz

Turok I (2014) Linking urbanisation and development in Africa's economic revival. In S Parnell and E Pieterse (eds) *Africa's Urban Revolution.* London: Zed

Tutu D (1999) *No Future Without Forgiveness.* New York: Doubleday

UN-Habitat (2010) *State of the World's Cities 2010/2011: Cities for All, Bridging the Urban Divide.* Nairobi

Van den Heuvel H (2008) 'Hidden messages' emerging from Afrocentric management perspectives. *Acta Commercii* 8: 41–54

Van Zwanenberg RM and King A (1975) *An Economic History of Kenya and Uganda 1800–1970.* London: Macmillan

Watson V (2009) 'The planned city sweeps the poor away...': Urban planning and 21st-century urbanisation. *Progress in Planning* 72(3): 151–193

Watson V and Agbola B (2013) *Who Will Plan African Cities?* London: African Research Institute

Wegerif M (2014) Exploring sustainable urban food provisioning: The case of eggs in Dar es Salaam. *Sustainability* 6(6): 3747–3779

Westermann D (1949) *The African Today and Tomorrow*. Oxford: Oxford University Press.

Yiftachel O (2009) Theoretical notes on 'gray cities': The coming of urban apartheid? *Planning Theory* 8(1): 88–100

Interviews (conducted in 2015)

Ignatius Gacheru, elder

Mwalimu Gacheru, Nguna

Mzee Richard Gitau, farmer and former member of the Mau Mau liberation movement, Githinguri

Gitu Wa Kahengeri, secretary-general of Mau Mau War Veterans Association, Gatuanyaga, Thika

Deborah Kinuthia, elder

Mama Nguyai, Kairi Village

Philomena Njeri Mbari, elder

Edith Muhindi, elder

Charles Rubia, Nairobi's first African mayor

Claudio Torres, UN-Habitat consultant, Nairobi

Njogu Wanguu, elder

Secretary of Kamukunji Jua Kali Association, Nairobi

Various workers at markets in Nairobi

About the author

MARY NJERI KINYANJUI is a writer, researcher, teacher and volunteer community organiser. She is a firm believer in social and economic justice and self-reliance. She holds a PhD in Geography from Fitzwilliam College at the University of Cambridge in the UK and is a senior research fellow at the University of Nairobi's Institute for Development Studies. At the time of writing, she was a visiting associate at the Five College Womens' Studies Research Center in Mount Holyoke, Massachusetts.

She has researched economic informality and small businesses, with particular focus on the role of grassroots and indigenous institutions, as well as gender, trade justice and peasant organisations, in the organisation of economic behaviour. Her current research is on the positioning of women peasants, artisans and traders in the global economy. Her publications include *Coffee Time* (Langaa), *Women and the Informal Economy in Urban Africa: From the Margins to the Center* (Zed) and *Vyama Institutions of Hope: Ordinary People's Market Coordination and Society Organization* (Nsemia).

9 781928 331780